THE PROCLAMATION OF BAHÁ'U'LLÁH

The Proclamation of
BAHÁ'U'LLÁH
to the kings and leaders of the world

"The time fore-ordained unto the peoples and kindreds of the earth is now come."

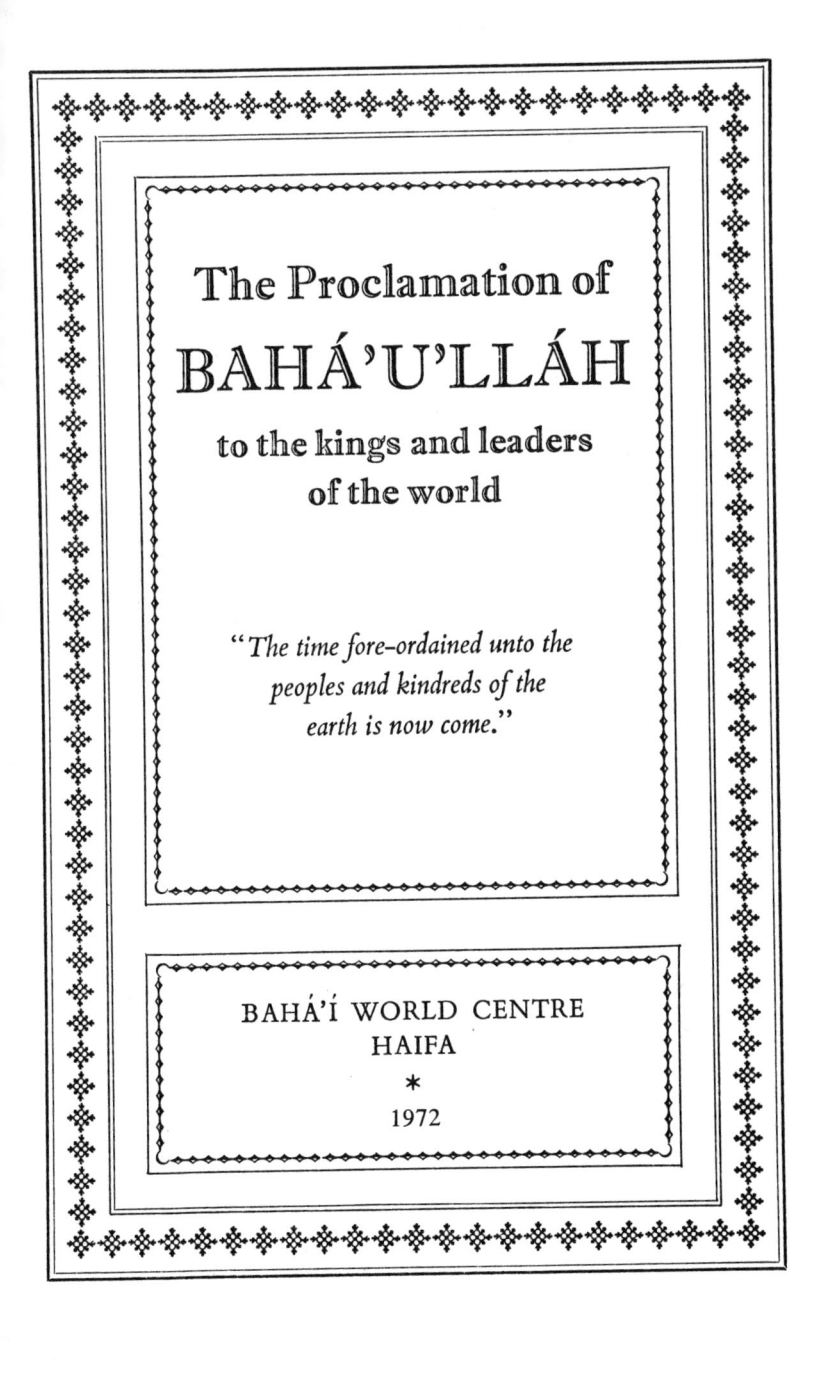

BAHÁ'Í WORLD CENTRE
HAIFA
*
1972

© UNIVERSAL HOUSE OF JUSTICE 1967
COPYRIGHT UNDER THE BERNE CONVENTION

SECOND IMPRESSION 1972

PRINTED IN THE UNITED STATES OF AMERICA

We desire but the good of the world and the happiness of the nations; yet they deem Us a stirrer up of strife and sedition worthy of bondage and banishment. . . . That all nations should become one in faith and all men as brothers; that the bonds of affection and unity between the sons of men should be strengthened; that diversity of religion should cease, and differences of race be annulled—what harm is there in this? . . . Yet so it shall be; these fruitless strifes, these ruinous wars shall pass away, and the 'Most Great Peace' shall come. . . . Yet do We see your kings and rulers lavishing their treasures more freely on means for the destruction of the human race than on that which would conduce to the happiness of mankind. . . . These strifes and this bloodshed and discord must cease, and all men be as one kindred and one family. . . . Let not a man glory in this, that he loves his country; let him rather glory in this, that he loves his kind. . . .

Contents

	Page
INTRODUCTION	ix
SUMMONS TO THE KINGS AND RULERS OF THE WORLD	1
Collectively	3
Napoleon III	15
Czar Alexander II	25
Queen Victoria	31
Kaiser Wilhelm I	37
Emperor Francis Joseph	41
Sulṭán 'Abdu'l-'Azíz	45
Náṣiri'd-Dín Sháh	55
The Rulers of America	61
The Elected Representatives of the People	65
SUMMONS TO THE WORLD'S RELIGIOUS LEADERS	69
Collectively	71
Pope Pius IX	81
The Clergy and People of Various Faiths	87
THE GREAT ANNOUNCEMENT TO MANKIND	109
REFERENCES	123

Introduction

ONE HUNDRED years ago, Bahá'u'lláh, Founder of the Bahá'í Faith, proclaimed in clear and unmistakable language, to the kings and rulers of the world, to its religious leaders, and to mankind in general that the long-promised age of world peace and brotherhood had at last dawned and that He Himself was the Bearer of the new message and power from God which would transform the prevailing system of antagonism and enmity between men and create the spirit and form of the destined world order.

At that time the splendour and panoply of the monarchs reflected the vast power which they exercised, autocratically for the most part, over the greater portion of the earth. Bahá'u'lláh, an exile from His native Persia for His religious teaching, was the prisoner of the tyrannical, all-powerful Sulṭán of the Ottoman Empire. In such circumstances He addressed the rulers of the world. His Tablets to particular kings and to the Pope, although delivered, were either ignored or rejected, their wise counsels and dire warnings went unheeded, and in one instance the bearer was cruelly tortured and killed.

Bahá'u'lláh, viewing that old world and seeing it 'at the mercy of rulers so drunk with pride that they cannot discern clearly their own best advantage' declared that '. . . the strife that divides and afflicts the human race is daily increasing. The signs of impending convulsions and chaos can now be discerned, inasmuch as the prevailing order appears to be lamentably defective.' Although painting in sombre tones the 'divine chastisement' which would assail most of those rulers and engulf in ruin the peoples of the world, He nevertheless left no doubt about the outcome. 'Soon', He declared, 'will the present day order be rolled up and a new one spread out in its stead.' Since the ascension of Bahá'u'lláh in 1892, in the Holy Land, the rolling up of the old order has become the daily experience of mankind and no abatement of this process is discernible. The essence of Bahá'u'lláh's World Order is the unity of the human race. 'O ye children of men', He writes, 'the fundamental purpose animating the Faith of God and His Religion is to safeguard the interests and promote the unity of the human race...' And He warns, 'The well-being of mankind, its peace and security, are unattainable unless and until its unity is firmly established.' The achievement of this unity is Bahá'u'lláh's declared mission and the aim of all Bahá'í activity. Its outline and structure are indicated in the following passage from the writings of Shoghi Effendi, great-grandson of Bahá'u'lláh and Guardian of the Bahá'í Faith:

> The unity of the human race, as envisaged by Bahá'u'lláh, implies the establishment of a world commonwealth in which all nations, races, creeds and classes are closely and permanently united, and in which the autonomy of its state members and the personal freedom and initiative of the individuals that

INTRODUCTION

compose them are definitely and completely safeguarded. This commonwealth must, as far as we can visualize it, consist of a world legislature, whose members will, as the trustees of the whole of mankind, ultimately control the entire resources of all the component nations, and will enact such laws as shall be required to regulate the life, satisfy the needs and adjust the relationships of all races and peoples. A world executive, backed by an international Force, will carry out the decisions arrived at, and apply the laws enacted by, this world legislature, and will safeguard the organic unity of the whole commonwealth. A world tribunal will adjudicate and deliver its compulsory and final verdict in all and any disputes that may arise between the various elements constituting this universal system. A mechanism of world inter-communication will be devised, embracing the whole planet, freed from national hindrances and restrictions, and functioning with marvellous swiftness and perfect regularity. A world metropolis will act as the nerve centre of a world civilization, the focus towards which the unifying forces of life will converge and from which its energizing influences will radiate. A world language will either be invented or chosen from among the existing languages and will be taught in the schools of all the federated nations as an auxiliary to their mother tongue. A world script, a world literature, a uniform and universal system of currency, of weights and measures, will simplify and facilitate intercourse and understanding among the nations and races of mankind. In such a world society, science and religion, the two most potent forces in human life, will be reconciled, will co-operate, and will harmoniously develop. The press will, under such a system, while giving full scope to the expression of the diversified views and convictions of mankind, cease to be mischievously manipulated by vested interests, whether private or public, and will be liberated from the influence of contending governments and peoples. The economic resources of the world will be organized, its sources of raw materials will be tapped and fully utilized, its markets will be co-ordinated and developed, and the distribution of its products will be equitably regulated.

National rivalries, hatreds and intrigues will cease, and racial animosity and prejudice will be replaced by racial amity, understanding and co-operation. The causes of religious strife will be permanently removed, economic barriers and restrictions will be completely abolished, and the inordinate distinction between classes will be obliterated. Destitution on the one hand, and gross accumulation of ownership on the other, will disappear. The enormous energy dissipated and wasted on war, whether economic or political, will be consecrated to such ends as will extend the range of human inventions and technical development, to the

INTRODUCTION

increase of the productivity of mankind, to the extermination of disease, to the extension of scientific research, to the raising of the standard of physical health, to the sharpening and refinement of the human brain, to the exploitation of the unused and unsuspected resources of the planet, to the prolongation of human life, and to the furtherance of any other agency that can stimulate the intellectual, the moral, and spiritual life of the entire human race.

A world federal system, ruling the whole earth and exercising unchallengeable authority over its unimaginably vast resources, blending and embodying the ideals of both the East and the West, liberated from the curse of war and its miseries, and bent on the exploitation of all the available sources of energy on the surface of the planet, a system in which Force is made the servant of Justice, whose life is sustained by its universal recognition of one God and by its allegiance to one common Revelation—such is the goal towards which humanity, impelled by the unifying forces of life, is moving.

Bahá'u'lláh's message is one of hope, of love, of practical reconstruction. Today we reap the appalling results of our forebears' rejection of His divine call; but today there are new rulers, new people, who perchance may hear and avoid or mitigate the severity of impending catastrophe. It is with this hope and believing it to be its sacred duty, that the Universal House of Justice, the international governing body of the Bahá'í Faith, proclaims again, through publication of these selected passages, the essence of that mighty call of a century ago. In the same hope and belief the Bahá'ís throughout the world will do their utmost during this centenary period to bring to the attention of their fellow-men the redeeming fact of this new outpouring of divine guidance and love. We believe they will not labour in vain.

Haifa, 1967

SUMMONS TO THE KINGS AND RULERS OF THE WORLD

COLLECTIVELY

O KINGS of the earth! He Who is the sovereign Lord of all is come. The Kingdom is God's, the omnipotent Protector, the Self-Subsisting. Worship none but God, and, with radiant hearts, lift up your faces unto your Lord, the Lord of all names. This is a Revelation to which whatever ye possess can never be compared, could ye but know it. We see you rejoicing in that which ye have amassed from others, and shutting out yourselves from the worlds which naught except My Guarded Tablet can reckon. The treasures ye have laid up have drawn you far away from your ultimate objective. This ill beseemeth you, could ye but understand it. Wash your hearts from all earthly defilements, and hasten to enter the Kingdom of your Lord, the Creator of earth and heaven, Who caused the world to tremble, and all its peoples to wail, except them that have renounced all things and clung to that which the Hidden Tablet hath ordained....

O Kings of the earth! The Most Great Law hath been revealed in this Spot, this Scene of transcendent splendour. Every hidden thing hath been brought to light, by virtue of the Will of the Supreme Ordainer, He Who hath ushered in the Last Hour, through Whom the Moon hath been cleft, and every irrevocable decree expounded.

Ye are but vassals, O Kings of the earth! He Who is the King of kings hath appeared, arrayed in His most wondrous glory, and is summoning you unto Himself, the Help in Peril, the Self-Subsisting. Take heed lest pride deter you from recognizing the Source of Revelation; lest the things of this world shut you out as by a veil from Him Who is the Creator of heaven. Arise, and serve Him Who is the Desire of all nations, Who hath created you through a word from Him, and ordained you to be, for all time, the emblems of His sovereignty.

By the righteousness of God! It is not Our wish to lay hands on your kingdoms. Our mission is to seize and possess the hearts of men. Upon them the eyes of Bahá are fastened. To this testifieth the Kingdom of Names, could ye but comprehend it. Whoso followeth his Lord, will renounce the world and all that is therein; how much greater, then, must be the detachment of Him Who holdeth so august a station! Forsake your palaces, and haste ye to gain admittance into His Kingdom. This, indeed, will profit you both in this world and in the next. To this testifieth the Lord of the realm on high, did ye but know it.

How great is the blessedness that awaiteth the king who will arise to aid My Cause in My Kingdom, who will detach himself from all else but Me! Such a king is numbered with the companions of the Crimson Ark, the Ark which God hath prepared for the people of Bahá. All must glorify his name, must reverence his station, and aid him to unlock the cities with the keys of My Name, the omnipotent Protector of all that inhabit the visible and invisible kingdoms. Such a king is the very eye of mankind, the luminous ornament on the brow of creation, the fountainhead of blessings unto the whole world. Offer up, O people of Bahá, your substance, nay your very lives, for his assistance.

We have asked nothing from you. For the sake of God We, verily, exhort you, and will be patient as We have been patient in that which hath befallen Us at your hands, O concourse of kings!

O KINGS of the earth! Give ear unto the Voice of God, calling from this sublime, this fruit-laden Tree, that hath sprung out of the Crimson Hill, upon the holy Plain, intoning the words: 'There is none other God but He, the Mighty, the All-Powerful, the All-Wise.' ... Fear God, O concourse of kings, and suffer not yourselves to be deprived of this most sublime grace. Fling away, then, the things ye possess, and take fast hold on the Handle of God, the Exalted, the Great. Set your hearts towards the Face of God, and abandon that which your desires have bidden you to follow, and be not of those who perish. Relate unto them, O Servant, the story of 'Alí (the Báb), when He came unto them with truth, bearing His glorious and weighty Book, and holding in His hands a testimony and proof from God, and holy and blessed tokens from Him. Ye, however, O Kings, have failed to heed the Remembrance of God in His days and to be guided by the lights which arose and shone forth above the horizon of a resplendent Heaven. Ye examined not His Cause when so to do would have been better for you than all that the sun shineth upon, could ye but perceive it. Ye remained careless until the divines of Persia—those cruel ones—pronounced judgment against Him, and unjustly slew Him. His spirit ascended unto God, and the eyes of the inmates of Paradise and the angels that are nigh unto Him wept sore by reason of this cruelty. Beware that ye be not careless henceforth as ye have been careless aforetime. Return, then, unto God, your Maker, and be not of the heedless. . . . My face hath come forth from the veils, and shed its radiance upon all that is in heaven and on earth; and yet, ye turned not towards Him, notwithstanding that ye were created for Him, O concourse of kings! Follow, therefore, that which I speak unto you, and hearken unto it with your hearts, and be not of such as have turned aside. For your glory consisteth not in your sovereignty, but rather in your nearness unto God and your observance of His command as sent down in His holy and preserved Tablets. Should any one of you rule over the whole earth, and over all that lieth within it and upon it, its seas, its lands, its mountains, and its plains, and yet be not remembered by God, all these would profit him not, could ye but know it. . . . Arise, then, and make steadfast your feet, and make ye amends for that which hath escaped you, and set then yourselves towards His holy Court, on the shore of His mighty Ocean, so that the pearls of knowledge and wisdom, which God hath stored up within the shell of His radiant heart, may be revealed unto you.... Beware lest ye hinder the breeze of God from blowing over your hearts, the breeze through which the hearts of such as have turned unto Him can be quickened....

Beware not to deal unjustly with any one that appealeth to you, and entereth beneath your shadow. Walk ye in the fear of God, and be ye of them that lead a godly life. Rest not on your power, your armies, and treasures. Put your whole trust and confidence in God, Who hath created you, and seek ye His help in all your affairs. Succour cometh from Him alone. He succoureth whom He willeth with the hosts of the heavens and of the earth.

Know ye that the poor are the trust of God in your midst. Watch that ye betray not His trust, that ye deal not unjustly with them and that ye walk not in the ways of the treacherous. Ye will most certainly be called upon to answer for His trust on the day when the Balance of Justice shall be set, the day when unto every one shall be rendered his due, when the doings of all men, be they rich or poor, shall be weighed.

If ye pay no heed unto the counsels which, in peerless and unequivocal language, We have revealed in this Tablet, Divine chastisement shall assail you from every direction, and the sentence of His justice shall be pronounced against you. On that day ye shall have no power to resist Him, and shall recognize your own impotence. Have mercy on yourselves and on those beneath you, and judge ye between them according to the precepts prescribed by God in His most holy and exalted Tablet, a Tablet wherein He hath assigned to each and every thing its settled measure, in which He hath given, with distinctness, an explanation of all things, and which is in itself a monition unto them that believe in Him.

Examine Our Cause, inquire into the things that have befallen Us, and decide justly between Us and Our enemies, and be ye of them that act equitably towards their neighbours. If ye stay not the hand of the oppressor, if ye fail to safeguard the rights of the down-trodden, what right have ye then to vaunt yourselves among men? What is it of which ye can rightly boast? Is it on your food and your drink that ye pride yourselves, on the riches ye lay up in your treasuries, on the diversity and the cost of the ornaments with which ye deck yourselves? If true glory were to consist in the possession of such perishable things, then the earth on which ye walk must needs vaunt itself over you, because it supplieth you, and bestoweth upon you, these very things, by the decree of the Almighty. In its bowels are contained, according to what God hath ordained, all that ye possess. From it, as a sign of His mercy, ye derive your riches. Behold then your state, the thing in which ye glory! Would that ye could perceive it! Nay, By Him Who holdeth in His grasp the kingdom of the entire creation! Nowhere doth your true and abiding glory reside except in your firm adherence unto the precepts of God, your wholehearted observance of His laws, your resolution

SUMMONS TO THE KINGS AND RULERS

to see that they do not remain unenforced, and to pursue steadfastly the right course. . . .

Twenty years have passed, O Kings, during which We have, each day, tasted the agony of a fresh tribulation. No one of them that were before Us hath endured the things We have endured. Would that ye could perceive it! They that rose up against Us, have put Us to death, have shed Our blood, have plundered Our property, and violated Our honour. Though aware of most of Our afflictions, ye, nevertheless, have failed to stay the hand of the aggressor. For is it not your clear duty to restrain the tyranny of the oppressor, and to deal equitably with your subjects, that your high sense of justice may be fully demonstrated to all mankind?

God hath committed into your hands the reins of the government of the people, that ye may rule with justice over them, safeguard the rights of the down-trodden, and punish the wrong-doers. If ye neglect the duty prescribed unto you by God in His Book, your names shall be numbered with those of the unjust in His sight. Grievous, indeed, will be your error. Cleave ye to that which your imaginations have devised, and cast behind your backs the commandments of God, the Most Exalted, the Inaccessible, the All-Compelling, the Almighty? Cast away the things ye possess, and cling to that which God hath bidden you observe. Seek ye His grace, for he that seeketh it treadeth His straight Path. . . .

The day is approaching when God will have exalted His

Cause and magnified His testimony in the eyes of all who are in the heavens and all who are on the earth. Place, in all circumstances, Thy whole trust in Thy Lord, and fix Thy gaze upon Him, and turn away from all them that repudiate His truth. Let God, Thy Lord, be Thy sufficing Succourer and Helper. We have pledged Ourself to secure Thy triumph upon earth and to exalt Our Cause above all men, though no king be found who would turn his face towards Thee.

O KINGS of the earth! We see you increasing every year your expenditures, and laying the burden thereof on your subjects. This, verily, is wholly and grossly unjust. Fear the sighs and tears of this Wronged One, and lay not excessive burdens on your peoples. Do not rob them to rear palaces for yourselves; nay rather choose for them that which ye choose for yourselves. Thus We unfold to your eyes that which profiteth you, if ye but perceive. Your people are your treasures. Beware lest your rule violate the commandments of God, and ye deliver your wards to the hands of the robber. By them ye rule, by their means ye subsist, by their aid ye conquer. Yet, how disdainfully ye look upon them! How strange, how very strange!

Now that ye have refused the Most Great Peace, hold ye fast unto this, the Lesser Peace, that haply ye may in some degree better your own condition and that of your dependents.

O Rulers of the earth! Be reconciled among yourselves, that ye may need no more armaments save in a measure to safeguard your territories and dominions. Beware lest ye disregard the counsel of the All-Knowing, the Faithful.

Be united, O Kings of the earth, for thereby will the tempest of discord be stilled amongst you, and your people find rest, if ye be of them that comprehend. Should any one among you take up arms against another, rise ye all against him, for this is naught but manifest justice.

The one true God, exalted be His glory, hath ever regarded, and will continue to regard, the hearts of men as His own, His exclusive possession. All else, whether pertaining to land or sea, whether riches or glory, He hath bequeathed unto the kings and rulers of the earth. From the beginning that hath no beginning the ensign proclaiming the words 'He doeth whatsoever He willeth' hath been unfurled in all its splendour before His Manifestation. What mankind needeth in this day is obedience unto them that are in authority, and a faithful adherence to the cord of wisdom. The instruments which are essential to the immediate protection, the security and assurance of the human race have been entrusted to the hands, and lie in the grasp, of the governors of human society. This is the wish of God and His decree.... We cherish the hope that one of the kings of the earth will, for the sake of God, arise for the triumph of this wronged, this oppressed people. Such a king will be eternally extolled and glorified. God hath prescribed unto this people the duty of aiding whosoever will aid them, of serving his best interests, and of demonstrating to him their abiding loyalty. They who follow Me must strive, under all circumstances, to promote the welfare of whosoever will arise for the triumph of My Cause, and must at all times prove their devotion and fidelity unto him. Happy is the man that hearkeneth and observeth My counsel. Woe unto him that faileth to fulfil My wish.

NAPOLEON III

O KING of Paris! Tell the priest to ring the bells no longer. By God, the True One! The Most Mighty Bell hath appeared in the form of Him Who is the Most Great Name, and the fingers of the will of Thy Lord, the Most Exalted, the Most High, toll it out in the heaven of Immortality, in His name, the All-Glorious. Thus have the mighty verses of Thy Lord been again sent down unto thee, that thou mayest arise to remember God, the Creator of earth and heaven, in these days when all the tribes of the earth have mourned, and the foundations of the cities have trembled, and the dust of irreligion hath enwrapped all men, except such as God, the All-Knowing, the All-Wise, was pleased to spare. Say: He Who is the Unconditioned is come, in the clouds of light, that He may quicken all created things with the breeze of His Name, the Most Merciful, and unify the world, and gather all men around this Table which hath been sent down from heaven. Beware that ye deny not the favour of God after it hath been sent down unto you. Better is this for you than that which ye possess; for that which is yours perisheth, whilst that which is with God endureth. He, in truth, ordaineth what He pleaseth. Verily, the breezes of forgiveness have been wafted from the direction of your Lord, the God of Mercy; whoso turneth thereunto, shall be cleansed of his sins, and of all pain and sickness. Happy the man that hath turned towards them, and woe betide him that hath turned aside.

Wert thou to incline thine inner ear unto all created things, thou wouldst hear: 'The Ancient of Days is come in His great glory!' Everything celebrateth the praise of its Lord. Some have known God and remember Him; others remember Him, yet know Him not. Thus have We set down Our decree in a perspicuous Tablet.

Give ear, O King, unto the Voice that calleth from the Fire which burneth in this verdant Tree, on this Sinai which hath been raised above the hallowed and snow-white Spot, beyond the Everlasting City: 'Verily, there is none other God but Me, the Ever-Forgiving, the Most Merciful!' We, in truth, have sent Him Whom We aided with the Holy Spirit (Jesus Christ) that He may announce unto you this Light that hath shone forth from the horizon of the will of your Lord, the Most Exalted, the All-Glorious, and Whose signs have been revealed in the West. Set your faces towards Him (Bahá'u'lláh) on this Day which God hath exalted above all other days, and whereon the All-Merciful hath shed the splendour of His effulgent glory upon all who are in heaven and all who are on earth. Arise thou to serve God and help His Cause. He, verily, will assist thee with the hosts of the seen and unseen, and will set thee king over all that whereon the sun riseth. Thy Lord, in truth, is the All-Powerful, the Almighty.

The breezes of the Most Merciful have passed over all created things; happy the man that hath discovered their fragrance, and set himself towards them with a sound heart. Attire thy temple with the ornament of My Name, and thy tongue with remembrance of Me, and thine heart with love for Me, the Almighty, the Most High. We have desired for thee naught except that which is better for thee than what thou dost possess and all the treasures of the earth. Thy Lord, verily, is knowing, informed of all. Arise, in My Name, amongst My servants, and say: 'O ye peoples of the earth! Turn yourselves towards Him Who hath turned towards you. He, verily, is the Face of God amongst you, and His Testimony and His Guide unto you. He hath come to you with signs which none can produce.' The voice of the Burning Bush is raised in the midmost heart of the world, and the Holy Spirit calleth aloud among the nations: 'Lo, the Desired One is come with manifest dominion!'

O King! The stars of the heaven of knowledge have fallen, they who seek to establish the truth of My Cause through the things they possess, and who make mention of God in My Name. And yet, when I came unto them in My glory, they turned aside. They, indeed, are of the fallen. This is, truly, that which the Spirit of God (Jesus Christ) hath announced, when He came with truth unto you, He with Whom the Jewish doctors disputed, till at last they perpetrated what hath made the Holy Spirit to lament, and the tears of them that have near access to God to flow. . . .

O King! We heard the words thou didst utter in answer to the Czar of Russia, concerning the decision made regarding the war (Crimean War). Thy Lord, verily, knoweth, is informed of all. Thou didst say: 'I lay asleep upon my couch, when the cry of the oppressed, who were drowned in the Black Sea, wakened me.' This is what we heard thee say, and, verily, thy Lord is witness unto what I say. We testify that that which wakened thee was not their cry but the promptings of thine own passions, for We tested thee, and found thee wanting. Comprehend the meaning of My words, and be thou of the discerning. It is not Our wish to address thee words of condemnation, out of regard for the dignity We conferred upon thee in this mortal life. We, verily, have chosen courtesy, and made it the true mark of such as are nigh unto Him. Courtesy, is, in truth, a raiment which fitteth all men, whether young or old. Well is it with him that adorneth his temple therewith, and woe unto him who is deprived of this great bounty. Hadst thou been sincere in thy words, thou wouldst have not cast behind thy back the Book of God, when it was sent unto thee by Him Who is the Almighty, the All-Wise. We have proved thee through it, and found thee other than that which thou didst profess. Arise, and make amends for that which escaped thee. Ere long the world and all that thou possessest will perish, and the kingdom will remain unto God, thy Lord and the Lord of thy fathers of old. It behoveth thee not to conduct thine affairs according to the dictates of thy desires. Fear the sighs of this Wronged One, and shield Him from the darts of such as act unjustly.

For what thou hast done, thy kingdom shall be thrown into confusion, and thine empire shall pass from thine hands, as a punishment for that which thou hast wrought.

TABLET TO NAPOLEON III

Then wilt thou know how thou hast plainly erred. Commotions shall seize all the people in that land, unless thou arisest to help this Cause, and followest Him Who is the Spirit of God (Jesus Christ) in this, the Straight Path. Hath thy pomp made thee proud? By My Life! It shall not endure; nay, it shall soon pass away, unless thou holdest fast by this firm Cord. We see abasement hastening after thee, whilst thou art of the heedless. It behoveth thee when thou hearest His Voice calling from the seat of glory to cast away all that thou possessest, and cry out: 'Here am I, O Lord of all that is in heaven and all that is on earth!'

O King! We were in 'Iráq, when the hour of parting arrived. At the bidding of the King of Islám (Sultán of Turkey) We set Our steps in his direction. Upon Our arrival, there befell Us at the hands of the malicious that which the books of the world can never adequately recount. Thereupon the inmates of Paradise, and they that dwell within the retreats of holiness, lamented; and yet the people are wrapped in a thick veil! . . .

More grievous became Our plight from day to day, nay, from hour to hour, until they took Us forth from Our prison and made Us, with glaring injustice, enter the Most Great Prison. . . .

Know of a truth that your subjects are God's trust amongst you. Watch ye, therefore, over them as ye watch over your own selves. Beware that ye allow not wolves to become the shepherds of the fold, or pride and conceit to deter you from turning unto the poor and the desolate.

Arise thou, in My name, above the horizon of renunciation, and set, then, thy face towards the Kingdom, at the bidding of thy Lord, the Lord of strength and of might.

Adorn the body of Thy kingdom with the raiment of My name, and arise, then, to teach My Cause. Better is this for thee than that which thou possessest. God will, thereby, exalt thy name among all the kings. Potent is He over all things. Walk thou amongst men in the name of God, and by the power of His might, that thou mayest show forth His signs amidst the peoples of the earth....

Regard ye the world as a man's body, which is afflicted with divers ailments, and the recovery of which dependeth upon the harmonizing of all of its component elements. Gather ye around that which We have prescribed unto you, and walk not in the ways of such as create dissension. Meditate on the world and the state of its people. He, for Whose sake the world was called into being, hath been imprisoned in the most desolate of cities ('Akká), by reason of that which the hands of the wayward have wrought. From the horizon of His prison-city He summoneth mankind unto the Dayspring of God, the Exalted, the Great. Exultest thou over the treasures thou dost possess, knowing they shall perish? Rejoicest thou in that thou rulest a span of earth, when the whole world, in the estimation of the people of Bahá, is worth as much as the black in the eye of a dead ant? Abandon it unto such as have set their affections upon it, and turn thou unto Him Who is the Desire of the world. Whither are gone the proud and their palaces? Gaze thou into their tombs, that thou mayest profit by this example, inasmuch as We made it a lesson unto every beholder. Were the breezes of Revelation to seize thee, thou wouldst flee the world, and turn unto the Kingdom, and wouldst expend all thou possessest, that thou mayest draw nigh unto this sublime Vision.

CZAR ALEXANDER II

O CZAR of Russia! Incline thine ear unto the voice of God, the King, the Holy, and turn thou unto Paradise, the Spot wherein abideth He Who, among the Concourse on high, beareth the most excellent titles, and Who, in the kingdom of creation, is called by the name of God, the Effulgent, the All-Glorious. Beware lest thy desire deter thee from turning towards the face of thy Lord, the Compassionate, the Most Merciful. We, verily, have heard the thing for which thou didst supplicate thy Lord, whilst secretly communing with Him. Wherefore, the breeze of My loving-kindness wafted forth, and the sea of My mercy surged, and We answered thee in truth. Thy Lord, verily, is the All-Knowing, the All-Wise. Whilst I lay chained and fettered in the prison, one of thy ministers extended Me his aid. Wherefore hath God ordained for thee a station which the knowledge of none can comprehend except His knowledge. Beware lest thou barter away this sublime station... Beware lest thy sovereignty withhold thee from Him Who is the Supreme Sovereign. He, verily, is come with His Kingdom, and all the atoms cry aloud: 'Lo! The Lord is come in His great majesty!' He Who is the Father is come, and the Son (Jesus), in the holy vale, crieth out: 'Here am I, here am I, O Lord, My God!' whilst Sinai circleth round the House, and the Burning Bush calleth aloud: 'The All-Bounteous is come mounted upon the clouds! Blessed is he that draweth nigh unto Him, and woe betide them that are far away.'

Arise thou amongst men in the name of this all-compelling Cause, and summon, then, the nations unto God, the Exalted, the Great. Be thou not of them who called upon God by one of His names, but who, when He Who is the Object of all names appeared, denied Him and turned aside from Him, and, in the end, pronounced sentence against Him with manifest injustice. Consider and call thou to mind the days whereon the Spirit of God (Jesus) appeared, and Herod gave judgment against Him. God, however, aided Him with the hosts of the unseen, and protected Him with truth, and sent Him down unto another land, according to His promise. He, verily, ordaineth what He pleaseth. Thy Lord truly preserveth whom He willeth, be he in the midst of the seas, or in the maw of the serpent, or beneath the sword of the oppressor. . . .

Again I say: Hearken unto My Voice that calleth from My prison that it may acquaint thee with the things that have befallen My Beauty, at the hands of them that are the manifestations of My glory, and that thou mayest perceive how great hath been My patience, notwithstanding My might, and how immense My forbearance, notwithstanding My power. By My Life! Couldst thou but know the things sent down by My Pen, and discover the treasures of My Cause, and the pearls of My mysteries which lie hid in the seas of My names and in the goblets of My words, thou wouldst, in thy love for My name, and in thy longing for

TABLET TO CZAR ALEXANDER II

My glorious and sublime Kingdom, lay down thy life in My path. Know thou that though My body be beneath the swords of My foes, and My limbs be beset with incalculable afflictions, yet My spirit is filled with a gladness with which all the joys of the earth can never compare.

Set thine heart towards Him Who is the Point of adoration for the world, and say: O peoples of the earth! Have ye denied the One in Whose path He Who came with the truth, bearing the announcement of your Lord, the Exalted, the Great, suffered martyrdom? Say: This is an Announcement whereat the hearts of the Prophets and Messengers have rejoiced. This is the One Whom the heart of the world remembereth and is promised in the Books of God, the Mighty, the All-Wise. The hands of the Messengers were, in their desire to meet Me, upraised towards God, the Mighty, the Glorified. . . . Some lamented in their separation from Me, others endured hardships in My path, and still others laid down their lives for the sake of My Beauty, could ye but know it. Say: I, verily, have not sought to extol Mine Own Self, but rather God Himself were ye to judge fairly. Naught can be seen in Me except God and His Cause, could ye but perceive it. I am the One Whom the tongue of Isaiah hath extolled, the One with Whose name both the Torah and the Evangel were adorned. . . . Blessed be the king whose sovereignty hath withheld him not from his Sovereign, and who hath turned unto God with his heart. He, verily, is accounted of those that have attained unto that which God, the Mighty, the All-Wise hath willed. Ere long will such a one find himself numbered with the monarchs of the realms of the Kingdom. Thy Lord is, in truth, potent over all things. He giveth what He willeth to whomsoever He willeth, and withholdeth what He pleaseth from whomsoever He willeth. He, verily, is the All-Powerful, the Almighty.

QUEEN VICTORIA

QUEEN in London! Incline thine ear unto the voice of thy Lord, the Lord of all mankind, calling from the Divine Lote-Tree: Verily, no God is there but Me, the Almighty, the All-Wise! Cast away all that is on earth, and attire the head of thy kingdom with the crown of the remembrance of thy Lord, the All-Glorious. He, in truth, hath come unto the world in His most great glory, and all that hath been mentioned in the Gospel hath been fulfilled. The land of Syria hath been honoured by the footsteps of its Lord, the Lord of all men, and North and South are both inebriated with the wine of His presence. Blessed is the man that inhaled the fragrance of the Most Merciful, and turned unto the Dawning-Place of His Beauty, in this resplendent Dawn. The Mosque of Aqṣá vibrateth through the breezes of its Lord, the All-Glorious whilst Baṭhá (Mecca) trembleth at the voice of God, the Exalted, the Most High. Whereupon every single stone of them celebrateth the praise of the Lord, through this Great Name.

Lay aside thy desire, and set then thine heart towards thy Lord, the Ancient of Days. We make mention of thee for the sake of God, and desire that thy name may be exalted through thy remembrance of God, the Creator of earth and heaven. He, verily, is witness unto that which I say. We have been informed that thou hast forbidden the trading in slaves, both men and women. This, verily, is what

God hath enjoined in this wondrous Revelation. God hath, truly, destined a reward for thee, because of this. He, verily, will pay the doer of good his due recompense, wert thou to follow what hath been sent unto thee by Him Who is the All-Knowing, the All-Informed. As to him who turneth aside, and swelleth with pride, after that the clear tokens have come unto him, from the Revealer of signs, his work shall God bring to naught. He, in truth, hath power over all things. Man's actions are acceptable after his having recognized (the Manifestation). He that turneth aside from the True One is indeed the most veiled amongst His creatures. Thus hath it been decreed by Him Who is the Almighty, the Most Powerful.

We have also heard that thou has entrusted the reins of counsel into the hands of the representatives of the people. Thou, indeed, hast done well, for thereby the foundations of the edifice of thine affairs will be strengthened, and the hearts of all that are beneath thy shadow, whether high or low, will be tranquillized. It behoveth them, however, to be trustworthy among His servants, and to regard themselves as the representatives of all that dwell on earth. This is what counselleth them, in this Tablet, He Who is the Ruler, the All-Wise... Blessed is he that entereth the assembly for the sake of God, and judgeth between men with pure justice. He, indeed, is of the blissful....

Turn thou unto God and say: O my Sovereign Lord! I am but a vassal of Thine, and Thou art, in truth, the King of Kings. I have lifted my suppliant hands unto the heaven of Thy grace and Thy bounties. Send down, then, upon me from the clouds of Thy generosity that which will rid me of all save Thee, and draw me nigh unto Thyself. I beseech Thee, O my Lord, by Thy name, which Thou hast made the king of names, and the manifestation of Thyself to all who are in heaven and on earth, to rend asunder the veils that have intervened between me and my recognition of the Dawning-Place of Thy signs and the Day Spring of Thy Revelation. Thou art, verily, the Almighty, the All-Powerful, the All-Bounteous. Deprive me not, O my Lord, of the fragrances of the Robe of Thy mercy in Thy days, and write down for me that which Thou hast written down for thy handmaidens who have believed in Thee and in Thy signs, and have recognized Thee, and set their hearts towards the horizon of Thy Cause. Thou art truly the Lord of the worlds and of those who show mercy the Most Merciful. Assist me, then, O my God, to remember Thee amongst Thy handmaidens, and to aid Thy Cause in Thy lands. Accept, then, that which hath escaped me when the light of Thy countenance shone forth. Thou, indeed, hast power over all things. Glory be to Thee, O Thou in Whose hand is the kingdom of the heavens and of the earth.

KAISER WILHELM I

O KING of Berlin! Give ear unto the Voice calling from this manifest Temple: Verily, there is none other God but Me, the Everlasting, the Peerless, the Ancient of Days. Take heed lest pride debar thee from recognizing the Dayspring of Divine Revelation, lest earthly desires shut thee out, as by a veil, from the Lord of the Throne above and of the earth below. Thus counselleth thee the Pen of the Most High. He, verily, is the Most Gracious, the All-Bountiful. Do thou remember the one whose power transcended thy power (Napoleon III), and whose station excelled thy station. Where is he? Whither are gone the things he possessed? Take warning, and be not of them that are fast asleep. He it was who cast the Tablet of God behind him, when We made known unto him what the hosts of tyranny had caused Us to suffer. Wherefore, disgrace assailed him from all sides, and he went down to dust in great loss. Think deeply, O King, concerning him, and concerning them who, like unto thee, have conquered cities and ruled over men. The All-Merciful brought them down from their palaces to their graves. Be warned, be of them who reflect... O banks of the Rhine! We have seen you covered with gore, inasmuch as the swords of retribution were drawn against you; and you shall have another turn. And We hear the lamentations of Berlin, though she be today in conspicuous glory.

EMPEROR FRANCIS JOSEPH

O EMPEROR of Austria! He who is the Dayspring of God's Light dwelt in the prison of 'Akká, at the time when thou didst set forth to visit the Aqṣá Mosque (Jerusalem). Thou passed Him by, and inquired not about Him, by Whom every house is exalted, and every lofty gate unlocked. We, verily, made it (Jerusalem) a place whereunto the world should turn, that they might remember Me, and yet thou hast rejected Him Who is the Object of this remembrance, when He appeared with the Kingdom of God, thy Lord and the Lord of the worlds. We have been with thee at all times, and found thee clinging unto the Branch and heedless of the Root. Thy Lord, verily, is a witness unto what I say. We grieved to see thee circle round Our Name, whilst unaware of Us, though We were before thy face. Open thine eyes, that thou mayest behold this glorious Vision, and recognize Him Whom thou invokest in the daytime and in the night-season, and gaze on the Light that shineth above this luminous Horizon.

SULṬÁN 'ABDU'L-'AZÍZ

HEARKEN, O King, to the speech of Him that speaketh the truth, Him that doth not ask thee to recompense Him with the things God hath chosen to bestow upon thee, Him Who unerringly treadeth the straight Path. He it is Who summoneth thee unto God, thy Lord, Who showeth thee the right course, the way that leadeth to true felicity, that haply thou mayest be of them with whom it shall be well.

Beware, O King, that thou gather not around thee such ministers as follow the desires of a corrupt inclination, as have cast behind their backs that which hath been committed into their hands and manifestly betrayed their trust. Be bounteous to others as God hath been bounteous to thee, and abandon not the interests of thy people to the mercy of such ministers as these. Lay not aside the fear of God, and be thou of them that act uprightly. Gather around thee those ministers from whom thou canst perceive the fragrance of faith and of justice, and take thou counsel with them, and choose whatever is best in thy sight, and be of them that act generously.

Know thou for a certainty that whoso disbelieveth in God is neither trustworthy nor truthful. This, indeed, is the truth, the undoubted truth. He that acteth treacherously towards God will, also, act treacherously towards his king. Nothing whatever can deter such a man from evil, nothing can hinder him from betraying his neighbour, nothing can induce him to walk uprightly.

Take heed that thou resign not the reins of the affairs of thy state into the hands of others, and repose not thy confidence in ministers unworthy of thy trust, and be not of them that live in heedlessness. Shun them whose hearts are turned away from thee, and place not thy confidence in them, and entrust them not with thy affairs and the affairs of such as profess thy faith. Beware that thou allow not the wolf to become the shepherd of God's flock, and surrender not the fate of His loved ones to the mercy of the malicious. Expect not that they who violate the ordinances of God will be trustworthy or sincere in the faith they profess. Avoid them, and preserve strict guard over thyself, lest their devices and mischief hurt thee. Turn away from them, and fix thy gaze upon God, thy Lord, the All-Glorious, the Most Bountiful. He that giveth up himself wholly to God, God shall, assuredly, be with him; and he that placeth his complete trust in God, God shall, verily, protect him from whatsoever may harm him, and shield him from the wickedness of every evil plotter.

Wert thou to incline thine ear unto My speech and observe My counsel, God would exalt thee to so eminent a position that the designs of no man on the whole earth could ever touch or hurt thee. Observe, O King, with thine inmost heart and with thy whole being, the precepts of God, and walk not in the paths of the oppressor. Seize thou, and hold firmly within the grasp of thy might, the

ADDRESS TO SULṬÁN ʿABDUʾL-ʿAZÍZ

reins of the affairs of thy people, and examine in person whatever pertaineth unto them. Let nothing escape thee, for therein lieth the highest good.

Render thanks unto God for having chosen thee out of the whole world, and made thee king over them that profess thy faith. It well beseemeth thee to appreciate the wondrous favours with which God hath favoured thee, and to magnify continually His name. Thou canst best praise Him if thou lovest His loved ones, and dost safeguard and protect His servants from the mischief of the treacherous, that none may any longer oppress them. Thou shouldst, moreover, arise to enforce the law of God amongst them, that thou mayest be of those who are firmly established in His law.

Shouldst thou cause rivers of justice to spread their waters amongst thy subjects, God would surely aid thee with the hosts of the unseen and of the seen and would strengthen thee in thine affairs. No God is there but Him. All creation and its empire are His. Unto Him return the works of the faithful.

Place not thy reliance on thy treasures. Put thy whole confidence in the grace of God, thy Lord. Let Him be thy trust in whatever thou doest, and be of them that have submitted themselves to His Will. Let Him be thy helper and enrich thyself with His treasures, for with Him are the treasuries of the heavens and of the earth. He bestoweth them upon whom He will, and from whom He will He withholdeth them. There is none other God but Him, the

All-Possessing, the All-Praised. All are but paupers at the door of His mercy; all are helpless before the revelation of His sovereignty, and beseech His favours.

Overstep not the bounds of moderation, and deal justly with them that serve thee. Bestow upon them according to their needs and not to the extent that will enable them to lay up riches for themselves, to deck their persons, to embellish their homes, to acquire the things that are of no benefit unto them, and to be numbered with the extravagant. Deal with them with undeviating justice, so that none among them may either suffer want, or be pampered with luxuries. This is but manifest justice.

Allow not the abject to rule over and dominate them who are noble and worthy of honour, and suffer not the high-minded to be at the mercy of the contemptible and worthless, for this is what We observed upon Our arrival in the City (Constantinople), and to it We bear witness. We found among its inhabitants some who were possessed of an affluent fortune and lived in the midst of excessive riches, whilst others were in dire want and abject poverty. This ill beseemeth thy sovereignty, and is unworthy of thy rank.

Let My counsel be acceptable to thee, and strive thou to rule with equity among men, that God may exalt thy name and spread abroad the fame of thy justice in all the world. Beware lest thou aggrandize thy ministers at the expense of thy subjects. Fear the sighs of the poor and of the upright in heart who, at every break of day, bewail their plight,

ADDRESS TO SULṬÁN ʿABDUʾL-ʿAZÍZ

and be unto them a benignant sovereign. They, verily, are thy treasures on earth. It behoveth thee, therefore, to safeguard thy treasures from the assaults of them who wish to rob thee. Inquire into their affairs, and ascertain, every year, nay every month, their condition, and be not of them that are careless of their duty.

Set before thine eyes God's unerring Balance and, as one standing in His Presence, weigh in that Balance thine actions every day, every moment of thy life. Bring thyself to account ere thou art summoned to a reckoning, on the Day when no man shall have strength to stand for fear of God, the Day when the hearts of the heedless ones shall be made to tremble.

It behoveth every king to be as bountiful as the sun, which fostereth the growth of all beings, and giveth to each its due, whose benefits are not inherent in itself, but are ordained by Him Who is the Most Powerful, the Almighty. The king should be as generous, as liberal in his mercy as the clouds, the outpourings of whose bounty are showered upon every land, by the behest of Him Who is the Supreme Ordainer, the All-Knowing.

Have a care not to entrust thine affairs of state entirely into another's hands. None can discharge thy functions better than thine own self. Thus do We make clear unto thee Our words of wisdom, and send down upon thee that which can enable thee to pass over from the left hand of oppression to the right hand of justice, and approach the resplendent ocean of His favours. Such is the path which the kings that were before thee have trodden, they that acted equitably towards their subjects, and walked in the ways of undeviating justice.

Thou art God's shadow on earth. Strive, therefore, to act in such a manner as befitteth so eminent, so august a station. If thou dost depart from following the things We have caused to descend upon thee and taught thee, thou wilt, assuredly, be derogating from that great and priceless honour. Return, then, and cleave wholly unto God, and cleanse thine heart from the world and all its vanities, and suffer not the love of any stranger to enter and dwell therein. Not until thou dost purify thine heart from every trace of such love can the brightness of the light of God shed its radiance upon it, for to none hath God given more than one heart. This, verily, hath been decreed and written down in His ancient Book. And as the human heart, as fashioned by God, is one and undivided, it behoveth thee to take heed that its affections be, also, one and undivided. Cleave thou, therefore, with the whole affection of thine heart, unto His love, and withdraw it from the love of any one besides Him, that He may aid thee to immerse thyself in the ocean of His unity, and enable thee to become a true upholder of His oneness. God is My witness. My sole purpose in revealing to thee these words is to sanctify thee from the transitory things of the earth, and aid thee to enter the realm of everlasting glory, that thou mayest, by the leave of God, be of them that abide and rule therein....

Let thine ear be attentive, O King, to the words We have

ADDRESS TO SULṬÁN ʿABDUʾL-ʿAZÍZ

addressed to thee. Let the oppressor desist from his tyranny, and cut off the perpetrators of injustice from among them that profess thy faith. By the righteousness of God! The tribulations We have sustained are such that any pen that recounteth them cannot but be overwhelmed with anguish. No one of them that truly believe and uphold the unity of God can bear the burden of their recital. So great have been Our sufferings that even the eyes of Our enemies have wept over Us, and beyond them those of every discerning person. And to all these trials have We been subjected, in spite of Our action in approaching thee, and in bidding the people to enter beneath thy shadow, that thou mightest be a stronghold unto them that believe in and uphold the unity of God.

Have I, O King, ever disobeyed thee? Have I, at any time, transgressed any of thy laws? Can any of thy ministers that represented thee in ʿIráq produce any proof that can establish my disloyalty to thee? No, by Him Who is the Lord of all worlds! Not for one short moment did We rebel against thee, or against any of thy ministers. Never, God willing, shall We revolt against thee, though We be exposed to trials more severe than any We suffered in the past.

In the day-time and in the night season, at even and at morn, We pray to God on thy behalf, that He may graciously aid thee to be obedient unto Him and to observe His commandment, that He may shield thee from the hosts of the evil ones. Do, therefore, as it pleaseth thee, and treat Us as befitteth thy station and beseemeth thy sovereignty. Be not forgetful of the law of God in whatever thou desirest to achieve, now or in the days to come. Say: Praise be to God, the Lord of all worlds!

NÁṢIRI'D-DÍN SHÁH

O KING! I was but a man like others, asleep upon My couch, when lo, the breezes of the All-Glorious were wafted over Me, and taught Me the knowledge of all that hath been. This thing is not from Me, but from One Who is Almighty and All-Knowing. And He bade Me lift up My voice between earth and heaven, and for this there befell Me what hath caused the tears of every man of understanding to flow. The learning current amongst men I studied not; their schools I entered not. Ask of the city wherein I dwelt, that thou mayest be well assured that I am not of them who speak falsely. This is but a leaf which the winds of the will of thy Lord, the Almighty, the All-Praised, have stirred. Can it be still when the tempestuous winds are blowing? Nay, by Him Who is the Lord of all Names and Attributes! They move it as they list. The evanescent is as nothing before Him Who is the Ever-Abiding. His all-compelling summons hath reached Me, and caused Me to speak His praise amidst all people. I was indeed as one dead when His behest was uttered. The hand of the will of thy Lord, the Compassionate, the Merciful, transformed Me. Can any one speak forth of his own accord that for which all men, both high and low, will protest against him? Nay, by Him Who taught the Pen the eternal mysteries, save him whom the grace of the Almighty, the All-Powerful, hath strengthened. The Pen of the Most High addresseth Me saying:

Fear not. Relate unto His Majesty the Sháh that which befell thee. His heart, verily, is between the fingers of thy Lord, the God of Mercy, that haply the sun of justice and bounty may shine forth above the horizon of his heart. Thus hath the decree been irrevocably fixed by Him Who is the All-Wise.

Look upon this Youth, O King, with the eyes of justice; judge thou, then, with truth concerning what hath befallen Him. Of a verity, God hath made thee His shadow amongst men, and the sign of His power unto all that dwell on earth. Judge thou between Us and them that have wronged Us without proof and without an enlightening Book. They that surround thee love thee for their own sakes, whereas this Youth loveth thee for thine own sake, and hath had no desire except to draw thee nigh unto the seat of grace, and to turn thee toward the right-hand of justice. Thy Lord beareth witness unto that which I declare.

O King! Wert thou to incline thine ear unto the shrill of the Pen of Glory and the cooing of the Dove of Eternity which, on the branches of the Lote-Tree beyond which there is no passing, uttereth praises to God, the Maker of all names and Creator of earth and heaven, thou wouldst attain unto a station from which thou wouldst behold in the world of being naught save the effulgence of the Adored One, and wouldst regard thy sovereignty as the most contemptible of thy possessions, abandoning it to whosoever might desire it, and setting thy face toward the Horizon aglow with the light of His countenance. Neither

TABLET TO NÁṢIRI'D-DÍN SHÁH

wouldst thou ever be willing to bear the burden of dominion save for the purpose of helping thy Lord, the Exalted, the Most High. Then would the Concourse on high bless thee. O how excellent is this most sublime station, couldst thou ascend thereunto through the power of a sovereignty recognized as derived from the Name of God! ...

O King of the age! The eyes of these refugees are turned towards and fixed upon the mercy of the Most Merciful. No doubt is there whatever that these tribulations will be followed by the outpourings of a supreme mercy, and these dire adversities be succeeded by an overflowing prosperity. We fain would hope, however, that His Majesty the Sháh will himself examine these matters, and bring hope to the hearts. That which We have submitted to thy Majesty is indeed for thine highest good. And God, verily, is a sufficient witness unto Me. ...

O would that thou wouldst permit Me, O Sháh, to send unto thee that which would cheer the eyes, and tranquillize the souls, and persuade every fair-minded person that with Him is the knowledge of the Book... But for the repudiation of the foolish and the connivance of the divines, I would have uttered a discourse that would have thrilled and carried away the hearts unto a realm from the murmur of whose winds can be heard: 'No God is there but He!' ...

I have seen, O Sháh, in the path of God what eye hath not seen nor ear heard... How numerous the tribulations which have rained, and will soon rain, upon Me! I advance with My face set towards Him Who is the Almighty, the All-Bounteous, whilst behind Me glideth the serpent. Mine eyes have rained down tears until My bed is drenched. I sorrow not for Myself, however. By God! Mine head yearneth for the spear out of love for its Lord. I never passed a tree, but Mine heart addressed it saying: 'O would that thou wert cut down in My name, and My body crucified upon thee, in the path of My Lord!'. . . By God! Though weariness lay Me low, and hunger consume Me, and the bare rock be My bed, and My fellows the beasts of the field, I will not complain, but will endure patiently as those endued with constancy and firmness have endured patiently, through the power of God, the Eternal King and Creator of the nations, and will render thanks unto God under all conditions. We pray that, out of His bounty—exalted be He—He may release, through this imprisonment, the necks of men from chains and fetters, and cause them to turn, with sincere faces, towards His Face, Who is the Mighty, the Bounteous. Ready is He to answer whosoever calleth upon Him, and nigh is He unto such as commune with Him.

THE RULERS OF AMERICA

HEARKEN ye, O Rulers of America and the Presidents of the Republics therein, unto that which the Dove is warbling on the Branch of Eternity: There is none other God but Me, the Ever-Abiding, the Forgiving, the All-Bountiful. Adorn ye the temple of dominion with the ornament of justice and of the fear of God, and its head with the crown of the remembrance of your Lord, the Creator of the heavens. Thus counselleth you He Who is the Dayspring of Names, as bidden by Him Who is the All-Knowing, the All-Wise. The Promised One hath appeared in this glorified Station, whereat all beings, both seen and unseen, have rejoiced. Take ye advantage of the Day of God. Verily, to meet Him is better for you than all that whereon the sun shineth, could ye but know it. O concourse of rulers! Give ear unto that which hath been raised from the Dayspring of Grandeur: Verily, there is none other God but Me, the Lord of Utterance, the All-Knowing. Bind ye the broken with the hands of justice, and crush the oppressor who flourisheth with the rod of the commandments of your Lord, the Ordainer, the All-Wise.

THE ELECTED REPRESENTATIVES
OF THE PEOPLE IN EVERY LAND

O YE the elected representatives of the people in every land! Take ye counsel together, and let your concern be only for that which profiteth mankind, and bettereth the condition thereof, if ye be of them that scan heedfully. Regard the world as the human body which, though at its creation whole and perfect, hath been afflicted, through various causes, with grave disorders and maladies. Not for one day did it gain ease, nay its sickness waxed more severe, as it fell under the treatment of ignorant physicians, who gave full rein to their personal desires, and have erred grievously. And if, at one time, through the care of an able physician, a member of that body was healed, the rest remained afflicted as before. Thus informeth you the All-Knowing, the All-Wise.

We behold it, in this day, at the mercy of rulers so drunk with pride that they cannot discern clearly their own best advantage, much less recognize a Revelation so bewildering and challenging as this. And whenever any one of them hath striven to improve its condition, his motive hath been his own gain, whether confessedly so or not; and the unworthiness of this motive hath limited his power to heal or cure.

That which the Lord hath ordained as the sovereign remedy and mightiest instrument for the healing of all the world is the union of all its peoples in one universal Cause, one common Faith. This can in no wise be achieved except through the power of a skilled, an all-powerful and inspired Physician. This, verily, is the truth, and all else naught but error. . . .

SUMMONS TO THE WORLD'S
RELIGIOUS LEADERS

COLLECTIVELY

O leaders of religion! Weigh not the Book of God with such standards and sciences as are current amongst you, for the Book itself is the unerring balance established amongst men. In this most perfect balance whatsoever the peoples and kindreds of the earth possess must be weighed, while the measure of its weight should be tested according to its own standard, did ye but know it.

The eye of My loving-kindness weepeth sore over you, inasmuch as ye have failed to recognize the One upon Whom ye have been calling in the daytime and in the night season, at even and at morn. Advance, O people, with snow-white faces and radiant hearts, unto the blest and crimson Spot, wherein the Sadratu'l-Muntahá is calling: 'Verily, there is none other God beside Me, the Omnipotent Protector, the Self-Subsisting!'

O ye leaders of religion! Who is the man amongst you that can rival Me in vision or insight? Where is he to be found that dareth to claim to be My equal in utterance or wisdom? No, by My Lord, the All-Merciful! All on the earth shall pass away; and this is the face of your Lord, the Almighty, the Well-Beloved.

We have decreed, O people, that the highest and last end of all learning be the recognition of Him Who is the Object of all knowledge; and yet, behold how ye have allowed your learning to shut you out, as by a veil, from Him Who is the Dayspring of this Light, through Whom every hidden thing hath been revealed. Could ye but discover the source whence the splendour of this utterance is diffused, ye would cast away the peoples of the world and all that they possess, and would draw nigh unto this most blessed Seat of glory.

Say: This, verily, is the heaven in which the Mother Book is treasured, could ye but comprehend it. He it is Who hath caused the Rock to shout, and the Burning Bush to lift up its voice, upon the Mount rising above the Holy Land, and proclaim: 'The Kingdom is God's, the sovereign Lord of all, the All-Powerful, the Loving!'

We have not entered any school, nor read any of your dissertations. Incline your ears to the words of this unlettered One, wherewith He summoneth you unto God, the Ever-Abiding. Better is this for you than all the treasures of the earth, could ye but comprehend it.

O CONCOURSE of divines! When My verses were sent down, and My clear tokens were revealed, We found you behind the veils. This, verily, is a strange thing. ... We have rent the veils asunder. Beware lest ye shut out the people by yet another veil. Pluck asunder the chains of vain imaginings, in the name of the Lord of all men, and be not of the deceitful. Should ye turn unto God, and embrace His

Cause, spread not disorder within it, and measure not the Book of God with your selfish desires. This, verily, is the counsel of God aforetime and hereafter.... Had ye believed in God, when He revealed Himself, the people would not have turned aside from Him, nor would the things ye witness today have befallen Us. Fear God, and be not of the heedless.... This is the Cause that hath caused all your superstitions and idols to tremble.... O concourse of divines! Beware lest ye be the cause of strife in the land, even as ye were the cause of the repudiation of the Faith in its early days. Gather the people around this Word that hath made the pebbles to cry out: 'The Kingdom is God's, the Dawning-Place of all signs!'... Tear the veils asunder in such wise that the inmates of the Kingdom will hear them being rent. This is the command of God, in days gone by, and for those to come. Blessed the man that observeth that whereunto he was bidden, and woe betide the negligent.

How long will ye, O concourse of divines, level the spears of hatred at the face of Bahá? Rein in your pens. Lo, the Most Sublime Pen speaketh betwixt earth and heaven. Fear God, and follow not your desires which have altered the face of creation. Purify your ears that they may hearken unto the Voice of God. By God! It is even as fire that consumeth the veils, and as water that washeth the souls of all who are in the universe.

O CONCOURSE of divines! Can any one of you race with the Divine Youth in the arena of wisdom and utterance, or soar with Him into the heaven of inner meaning and explanation? Nay, by My Lord, the God of mercy! All have swooned away in this Day from the Word of thy Lord. They are even as dead and lifeless, except him whom thy Lord, the Almighty, the Unconstrained, hath willed to exempt. Such a one is indeed of those endued with knowledge in the sight of Him Who is the All-Knowing. The inmates of Paradise, and the dwellers of the sacred Folds, bless him at eventide and at dawn. Can the one possessed of wooden legs resist him whose feet God hath made of steel? Nay, by Him Who illumineth the whole of creation!

WHEN We observed carefully, We discovered that Our enemies are, for the most part, the divines... Among the people are those who said: He hath repudiated the divines. Say: Yea, by My Lord! I, in very truth, was the One Who abolished the idols! We, verily, have sounded the Trumpet, which is Our Most Sublime Pen, and lo, the divines and the learned, and the doctors and the rulers, swooned away except such as God preserved, as a token of His grace, and He, verily, is the All-Bounteous, the Ancient of Days. . .

O concourse of divines! Fling away idle fancies and imaginings, and turn, then, towards the Horizon of Certitude. I swear by God! All that ye possess will profit you not, neither all the treasures of the earth, nor the leadership ye have usurped. Fear God, and be not of the lost ones. . . Say: O concourse of divines! Lay aside all your veils and coverings. Give ear unto that whereunto calleth you the Most Sublime Pen, in this wondrous Day. . . . The world is laden with dust, by reason of your vain imaginings, and the hearts of such as enjoy near access to God are troubled because of your cruelty. Fear God, and be of them that judge equitably.

O YE the dawning-places of knowledge! Beware that ye suffer not yourselves to become changed, for as ye change, most men will, likewise, change. This, verily, is an injustice unto yourselves and unto others. . . . Ye are even as a spring. If it be changed, so will the streams that branch out from it be changed. Fear God, and be numbered with the godly. In like manner, if the heart of man be corrupted, his limbs will also be corrupted. And similarly, if the root of a tree be corrupted, its branches, and its offshoots, and its leaves, and its fruits, will be corrupted. . . .

O concourse of divines! Be fair, I adjure you by God, and nullify not the Truth with the things ye possess. Peruse that which We have sent down with truth. It will, verily, aid you, and will draw you nigh unto God, the Mighty, the Great. Consider and call to mind how when Muḥammad, the Apostle of God, appeared, the people denied Him. They ascribed unto Him what caused the Spirit (Jesus) to lament in His Most Sublime Station, and the Faithful Spirit to cry out. Consider, moreover, the things which befell the Apostles and Messengers of God before Him, by reason of what the hands of the unjust have wrought. We make mention of you for the sake of God, and remind you of His signs, and announce unto you the things ordained for such as are nigh unto Him in the most sublime Paradise and the all-highest Heaven, and I, verily, am the Announcer, the Omniscient. He hath come for your salvation, and hath borne tribulations that ye may ascend, by the ladder of utterance, unto the summit of understanding. . . . Peruse, with fairness and justice, that which hath been sent down. It will, verily, exalt you through the truth, and will cause you to behold the things from which ye have been withheld, and will enable you to quaff His sparkling Wine.

SUMMONS TO THE WORLD'S RELIGIOUS LEADERS

Those divines... who are truly adorned with the ornament of knowledge and of a goodly character are, verily, as a head to the body of the world, and as eyes to the nations. The guidance of men hath, at all times, been and is dependent upon these blessed souls.

The divine whose conduct is upright, and the sage who is just, are as the spirit unto the body of the world. Well is it with that divine whose head is attired with the crown of justice, and whose temple is adorned with the ornament of equity.

The divine who hath seized and quaffed the most holy Wine, in the name of the sovereign Ordainer, is as an eye unto the world. Well is it with them who obey him, and call him to remembrance.

Great is the blessedness of that divine that hath not allowed knowledge to become a veil between him and the One Who is the Object of all knowledge, and who, when the Self-Subsisting appeared, hath turned with a beaming face towards Him. He, in truth, is numbered with the learned. The inmates of Paradise seek the blessing of his breath, and his lamp sheddeth its radiance over all who are in heaven and on earth. He, verily, is numbered with the inheritors of the Prophets. He that beholdeth him hath, verily, beheld the True One, and he that turneth towards him hath, verily, turned towards God, the Almighty, the All-Wise.

O CONCOURSE of divines! Ye shall not henceforth behold yourselves possessed of any power, inasmuch as We have seized it from you, and destined it for such as have believed in God, the One, the All-Powerful, the Almighty, the Unconstrained.

POPE PIUS IX

O pope! Rend the veils asunder. He Who is the Lord of Lords is come overshadowed with clouds, and the decree hath been fulfilled by God, the Almighty, the Unrestrained... He, verily, hath again come down from Heaven even as He came down from it the first time. Beware that thou dispute not with Him even as the Pharisees disputed with Him (Jesus) without a clear token or proof. On His right hand flow the living waters of grace, and on His left the choice Wine of justice, whilst before Him march the angels of Paradise, bearing the banners of His signs. Beware lest any name debar thee from God, the Creator of earth and heaven. Leave thou the world behind thee, and turn towards thy Lord, through Whom the whole earth hath been illumined... Dwellest thou in palaces whilst He Who is the King of Revelation liveth in the most desolate of abodes? Leave them unto such as desire them, and set thy face with joy and delight towards the Kingdom... Arise in the name of thy Lord, the God of Mercy, amidst the peoples of the earth, and seize thou the Cup of Life with the hands of confidence, and first drink thou therefrom, and proffer it then to such as turn towards it amongst the peoples of all faiths...

Call thou to remembrance Him Who was the Spirit (Jesus), Who when He came, the most learned of His age pronounced judgment against Him in His own country, whilst he who was only a fisherman believed in Him. Take heed, then, ye men of understanding heart! Thou, in truth, art one of the suns of the heaven of His names. Guard thyself, lest darkness spread its veils over thee, and fold thee away from His light... Consider those who opposed the Son (Jesus), when He came unto them with sovereignty and power. How many the Pharisees who were waiting to behold Him, and were lamenting over their separation from Him! And yet, when the fragrance of His coming was wafted over them, and His beauty was unveiled, they turned aside from Him and disputed with Him... None save a very few, who were destitute of any power amongst men, turned towards His face. And yet, today, every man endowed with power and invested with sovereignty prideth himself on His Name! In like manner, consider how numerous, in these days, are the monks who, in My Name, have secluded themselves in their churches, and who, when the appointed time was fulfilled, and We unveiled Our beauty, knew Us not, though they call upon Me at eventide and at dawn....

The Word which the Son concealed is made manifest. It hath been sent down in the form of the human temple in this day. Blessed be the Lord Who is the Father! He, verily, is come unto the nations in His most great majesty. Turn your faces towards Him, O concourse of the righteous... This is the day whereon the Rock (Peter) crieth out and shouteth, and celebrateth the praise of its Lord, the All-Possessing, the Most High, saying: 'Lo! The Father is come, and that which ye were promised in the Kingdom is fulfilled! . . .' My body longeth for the cross, and Mine head waiteth the thrust of the spear, in the path of the All-Merciful, that the world may be purged from its transgressions. . . .

O Supreme Pontiff! Incline thine ear unto that which the Fashioner of mouldering bones counselleth thee, as voiced by Him Who is His Most Great Name. Sell all the embellished ornaments thou dost possess, and expend them in the path of God, Who causeth the night to return upon the day, and the day to return upon the night. Abandon thy kingdom unto the kings, and emerge from thy habitation, with thy face set towards the Kingdom, and, detached from the world, then speak forth the praises of thy Lord betwixt earth and heaven. Thus hath bidden thee He Who is the Possessor of Names, on the part of thy Lord, the Almighty, the All-Knowing. Exhort thou the kings and say: 'Deal equitably with men. Beware lest ye transgress the bounds fixed in the Book.' This indeed becometh thee. Beware lest thou appropriate unto thyself the things of the world and the riches thereof. Leave them unto such as desire them, and cleave unto that which hath been enjoined upon thee by Him Who is the Lord of creation. Should any one offer thee all the treasures of the earth, refuse to even glance upon them. Be as thy Lord hath been. Thus hath the Tongue of Revelation spoken that which God hath made the ornament of the book of creation. . . Should the inebriation of the wine of My verses seize thee, and thou determinest to present thyself before the throne of thy Lord, the Creator of earth and heaven, make My love thy vesture and thy shield remembrance of Me, and thy provision reliance upon God, the Revealer of all power... Verily, the day of ingathering is come, and all things have been separated from each other. He hath stored away that which He chose in the vessels of justice, and cast into fire that which befitteth it. Thus hath it been decreed by your Lord, the Mighty, the Loving, in this promised Day. He, verily, ordaineth what He pleaseth. There is none other God save He, the Almighty, the All-Compelling.

THE CLERGY AND PEOPLE OF VARIOUS FAITHS

At one time We address the people of the Torah and summon them unto Him Who is the Revealer of verses, Who hath come from Him Who layeth low the necks of men. . . . At another, We address the people of the Evangel and say: 'The All-Glorious is come in this Name whereby the Breeze of God hath wafted over all regions.'. . . . At still another, We address the people of the Qur'án saying: 'Fear the All-Merciful, and cavil not at Him through Whom all religions were founded.'. . . . Know thou, moreover, that We have addressed to the Magians Our Tablets, and adorned them with Our Law. . . . We have revealed in them the essence of all the hints and allusions contained in their Books. The Lord, verily, is the Almighty, the All-Knowing.

Call out to Zion, O Carmel, and announce the joyful tidings: He that was hidden from mortal eyes is come! His all-conquering sovereignty is manifest; His all-encompassing splendour is revealed. Beware lest thou hesitate or halt. Hasten forth and circumambulate the City of God that hath descended from heaven, the celestial Kaaba round which have circled in adoration the favoured of God, the pure in heart, and the company of the most exalted angels. O how I long to announce unto every spot on the surface of the earth, and to carry to each one of its cities, the glad-tidings of this Revelation—a Revelation to which the heart of Sinai hath been attracted, and in whose name the Burning Bush is calling: 'Unto God, the Lord of Lords, belong the kingdoms of earth and heaven.' Verily this is the Day in which both land and sea rejoice at this announcement, the Day for which have been laid up those things which God, through a bounty beyond the ken of mortal mind or heart, hath destined for revelation. Ere long will God sail His Ark upon thee, and will manifest the people of Bahá who have been mentioned in the Book of Names.

The Most Great Law is come, and the Ancient Beauty ruleth upon the throne of David. Thus hath My Pen spoken that which the histories of bygone ages have related. At this time, however, David crieth aloud and saith: 'O my loving Lord! Do Thou number me with such as have stood steadfast in Thy Cause, O Thou through Whom the faces have been illumined, and the footsteps have slipped!'

The Breath hath been wafted, and the Breeze hath blown, and from Zion hath appeared that which was hidden, and from Jerusalem is heard the Voice of God, the One, the Incomparable, the Omniscient.

Lend an ear unto the song of David. He saith: 'Who will bring me into the Strong City?' The Strong City is 'Akká, which hath been named the Most Great Prison, and which possesseth a fortress and mighty ramparts... Peruse that which Isaiah hath spoken in His Book. He saith: 'Get thee up into the high mountain, O Zion, that bringest good tidings; lift up thy voice with strength, O Jerusalem, that bringest good tidings. Lift it up, be not afraid; say unto the cities of Judah: 'Behold your God! Behold the Lord God will come with strong hand, and His arm shall rule for Him.' This Day all the signs have appeared. A great City hath descended from heaven, and Zion trembleth and exulteth with joy at the Revelation of God, for it hath heard the Voice of God on every side.

O CONCOURSE of Christians! We have, on a previous occasion, revealed Ourself unto you, and ye recognized Me not. This is yet another occasion vouchsafed unto you. This is the Day of God; turn ye unto Him... The Beloved One loveth not that ye be consumed with the fire of your desires. Were ye to be shut out as by a veil from Him, this would be for no other reason than your own waywardness and ignorance. Ye make mention of Me, and know Me not. Ye call upon Me, and are heedless of My Revelation.... O people of the Gospel! They who were not in the Kingdom have now entered it, whilst We behold you, in this day, tarrying at the gate. Rend the veils asunder by the power of your Lord, the Almighty, the All-Bounteous, and enter, then, in My name My Kingdom. Thus biddeth you He Who desireth for you everlasting life... We behold you, O children of the Kingdom, in darkness. This, verily, beseemeth you not. Are ye, in the face of the Light, fearful because of your deeds? Direct yourselves towards Him... Verily, He (Jesus) said: 'Come ye after Me, and I will make you to become fishers of men.' In this day, however, We say: 'Come ye after Me, that We may make you to become quickeners of mankind.'

We, verily, have come for your sakes, and have borne the misfortunes of the world for your salvation. Flee ye the One Who hath sacrificed His life that ye may be quickened? Fear God, O followers of the Spirit (Jesus), and walk not in the footsteps of every divine that hath gone far astray... Open the doors of your hearts. He Who is the Spirit (Jesus) verily, standeth before them. Wherefore keep ye afar from Him Who hath purposed to draw you nigh unto a Resplendent Spot? Say: We, in truth, have opened unto you the gates of the Kingdom. Will ye bar the doors of your houses in My face? This indeed is naught but a grievous error.

O CONCOURSE of patriarchs! He Whom ye were promised in the Tablets is come. Fear God, and follow not the vain imaginings of the superstitious. Lay aside the things ye possess, and take fast hold of the Tablet of God by His sovereign power. Better is this for you than all your possessions. Unto this testifieth every understanding heart, and every man of insight. Pride ye yourselves on My Name and yet shut yourselves out as by a veil from Me? This indeed is a strange thing!

THE CLERGY AND PEOPLE OF VARIOUS FAITHS

O CONCOURSE of archbishops! He Who is the Lord of all men hath appeared. In the plain of guidance He calleth mankind, whilst ye are numbered with the dead! Great is the blessedness of him who is stirred by the Breeze of God, and hath arisen from amongst the dead in this perspicuous Name.

O CONCOURSE of bishops! Trembling hath seized all the kindreds of the earth, and He Who is the Everlasting Father calleth aloud between earth and heaven. Blessed the ear that hath heard, and the eye that hath seen, and the heart that hath turned unto Him Who is the Point of Adoration of all who are in the heavens and all who are on earth. . . .

O CONCOURSE of bishops! Ye are the stars of the heaven of My knowledge. My mercy desireth not that ye should fall upon the earth. My justice, however, declareth: 'This is that which the Son (Jesus) hath decreed.' And whatsoever hath proceeded out of His blameless, His truth-speaking, trustworthy mouth, can never be altered. The bells, verily, peal out My Name, and lament over Me, but My spirit rejoiceth with evident gladness. The body of the Loved

One yearneth for the cross, and His head is eager for the spear, in the path of the All-Merciful. The ascendancy of the oppressor can in no wise deter Him from His purpose... The stars of the heaven of knowledge have fallen, they that adduce the proofs they possess in order to demonstrate the truth of My Cause, and who make mention of God in My name. When I came unto them, in My majesty, however, they turned aside from Me. They, verily, are of the fallen. This is what the Spirit (Jesus) prophesied when He came with the truth, and the Jewish doctors cavilled at Him, until they committed what made the Holy Spirit to lament, and the eyes of such as enjoy near access to God to weep.

O CONCOURSE of priests! Leave the bells, and come forth, then, from your churches. It behoveth you, in this day, to proclaim aloud the Most Great Name among the nations. Prefer ye to be silent, whilst every stone and every tree shouteth aloud: 'The Lord is come in His great glory!' ... He that summoneth men in My name is, verily, of Me, and he will show forth that which is beyond the power of all that are on earth... Let the Breeze of God awaken you. Verily, it hath wafted over the world. Well is it with him that hath discovered the fragrance thereof and been accounted among the well-assured....

THE CLERGY AND PEOPLE OF VARIOUS FAITHS

O CONCOURSE of priests! The Day of Reckoning hath appeared, the Day whereon He Who was in heaven hath come. He, verily, is the One Whom ye were promised in the Books of God, the Holy, the Almighty, the All-Praised. How long will ye wander in the wilderness of heedlessness and superstition? Turn with your hearts in the direction of your Lord, the Forgiving, the Generous.

O CONCOURSE of monks! Seclude not yourselves in churches and cloisters. Come forth by My leave, and occupy yourselves with that which will profit your souls and the souls of men. Thus biddeth you the King of the Day of Reckoning. Seclude yourselves in the stronghold of My love. This, verily, is a befitting seclusion, were ye of them that perceive it. He that shutteth himself up in a house is indeed as one dead. It behoveth man to show forth that which will profit all created things, and he that bringeth forth no fruit is fit for fire. Thus counselleth you your Lord, and He, verily, is the Almighty, the All-Bounteous. Enter ye into wedlock, that after you someone may fill your place. We have forbidden you perfidious acts, and not that which will demonstrate fidelity. Have ye clung to the standards fixed by your own selves, and cast the standards of God behind your backs? Fear God, and be not of the foolish. But for man, who would make mention of Me on My earth, and how could My attributes and My name have been revealed? Ponder ye, and be not of them that are veiled and fast asleep. He that wedded not (Jesus) found no place wherein to dwell or lay His head, by reason of that which the hands of the treacherous had wrought. His sanctity consisteth not in that which ye believe or fancy, but rather in the things We possess. Ask, that ye may apprehend His station which hath been exalted above the imaginings of all that dwell on earth. Blessed are they who perceive it.

O CONCOURSE of monks! If ye choose to follow Me, I will make you heirs of My Kingdom; and if ye transgress against Me, I will, in My long-suffering, endure it patiently, and I, verily, am the Ever-Forgiving, the All-Merciful. . . Bethlehem is astir with the Breeze of God. We hear her voice saying: 'O most generous Lord! Where is Thy great glory established? The sweet savours of Thy presence have quickened me, after I had melted in my separation from Thee. Praised be Thou in that Thou hast raised the veils, and come with power in evident glory.' We called unto her from behind the Tabernacle of Majesty and Grandeur: 'O Bethlehem! This Light hath risen in the orient, and travelled towards the occident, until it reached thee in the evening of its life. Tell Me then: Do the sons recognize the Father, and acknowledge Him, or do they deny Him, even as the people aforetime denied Him (Jesus)?' Whereupon she cried out saying: 'Thou art, in truth, the All-Knowing, the Best-Informed.'

Consider, likewise, how numerous at this time are the monks who have secluded themselves in their churches, in My name, and who, when the appointed time came, and We unveiled to them Our beauty, failed to recognize Me, notwithstanding that they call upon Me at dawn and at eventide.

Read ye the Evangel and yet refuse to acknowledge the All-Glorious Lord? This indeed beseemeth you not, O concourse of learned men!... The fragrances of the All-Merciful have wafted over all creation. Happy the man that hath forsaken his desires, and taken fast hold of guidance.

Perused ye not the Qur'án? Read it, that haply ye may find the Truth, for this Book is verily the Straight Path. This is the Way of God unto all who are in the heavens and all who are on the earth. If ye have been careless of the Qur'án, the Bayán cannot be regarded to be remote from you. Behold it open before your eyes. Read ye its verses, lest perchance ye desist from committing that which will cause the Messengers of God to mourn and lament.

Speed out of your sepulchres. How long will ye sleep? The second blast hath been blown on the trumpet. On whom are ye gazing? This is your Lord, the God of Mercy. Witness how ye gainsay His signs! The earth hath quaked with a great quaking, and cast forth her burdens. Will ye not admit it? Say: Will ye not recognize how the mountains have become like flocks of wool, how the people are sore vexed at the awful majesty of the Cause of God? Witness how their houses are empty ruins, and they themselves a drowned host.

This is the Day whereon the All-Merciful hath come down in the clouds of knowledge, clothed with manifest sovereignty. He well knoweth the actions of men. He it is Whose glory none can mistake, could ye but comprehend it. The heaven of every religion hath been rent, and the earth of human understanding been cleft asunder, and the angels of God are seen descending. Say: This is the Day of mutual deceit; whither do ye flee? The mountains have passed away, and the heavens have been folded together, and the whole earth is held within His grasp, could ye but understand it. Who is it that can protect you? None, by Him Who is the All-Merciful! None, except God, the Almighty, the All-Glorious, the Beneficent. Every woman that hath had a burden in her womb hath cast her burden. We see men drunken in this Day, the Day in which men and angels have been gathered together.

Is there any doubt concerning God? Behold how He hath come down from the heaven of His grace, girded with power and invested with sovereignty. Is there any doubt concerning His signs? Open ye your eyes, and consider His clear evidence. Paradise is on your right hand, and hath been brought nigh unto you, while Hell hath been made to blaze. Witness its devouring flame. Haste ye to enter into Paradise, as a token of Our mercy unto you, and drink ye from the hands of the All-Merciful the Wine that is life indeed.

By Him Who is the Great Announcement! The All-Merciful is come invested with undoubted sovereignty. The Balance hath been appointed, and all them that dwell on earth have been gathered together. The Trumpet hath been blown, and lo, all eyes have stared up with terror, and the hearts of all who are in the heavens and on the earth have trembled, except them whom the breath of the verses of God hath quickened, and who have detached themselves from all things.

This is the Day whereon the earth shall tell out her tidings. The workers of iniquity are her burdens, could ye but perceive it. The moon of idle fancy hath been cleft, and the heaven hath given out a palpable smoke. We see the people laid low, awed with the dread of thy Lord, the Almighty, the Most Powerful. The Crier hath cried out, and men have been torn away, so great hath been the fury of His wrath. The people of the left hand sigh and bemoan. The people of the right abide in noble habitations: they quaff the Wine that is life indeed, from the hands of the All-Merciful, and are, verily, the blissful.

The earth hath been shaken, and the mountains have passed away, and the angels have appeared, rank on rank, before Us. Most of the people are bewildered in their drunkenness and wear on their faces the evidences of anger. Thus have We gathered together the workers of iniquity. We see them rushing on towards their idol. Say: None shall be secure this Day from the decree of God. This indeed is a grievous Day. We point out to them those that led them astray. They see them, and yet recognize them not. Their eyes are drunken; they are indeed a blind people. Their proofs are the calumnies they uttered; condemned are their calumnies by God, the Help in Peril, the Self-Subsisting. The Evil One hath stirred up mischief in their hearts, and they are afflicted with a torment that none can avert. They hasten to the wicked, bearing the register of the workers of iniquity. Such are their doings.

Say: The heavens have been folded together, and the earth is held within His grasp, and the corrupt doers have been held by their forelock, and still they understand not. They drink of the tainted water, and know it not. Say: The shout hath been raised, and the people have come forth from their graves, and arising are gazing around them. Some have made haste to attain the court of the God of Mercy, others have fallen down on their faces in the fire of Hell, while still others are lost in bewilderment. The verses of God have been revealed, and yet they have turned away from them. His proof hath been manifested and yet they are unaware of it. And when they behold the face of the All-Merciful, their own faces are saddened, while they are disporting themselves. They hasten forward to Hell Fire, and mistake it for light. Far from God be what they fondly imagine! Say: Whether ye rejoice or whether ye burst for fury, the heavens are cleft asunder, and God hath come down, invested with radiant sovereignty. All created things are heard exclaiming: 'The Kingdom is God's, the Almighty, the All-Knowing, the All-Wise.'

O CONCOURSE of Persian divines! In My name ye have seized the reins of men, and occupy the seats of honour by reason of your relation to Me. When I revealed Myself, however, ye turned aside, and committed what hath caused the tears of such as have recognized Me to flow. Erelong will all that ye possess perish, and your glory be turned into the most wretched abasement, and ye shall behold the punishment for what ye have wrought, as decreed by God, the Ordainer, the All-Wise.

O YE divines of the City! We came to you with the truth, whilst ye were heedless of it. Methinks ye are as dead, wrapt in the coverings of your own selves. Ye sought not Our presence, when so to do would have been better for you than all your doings. . . . Know ye, that had your leaders, to whom ye owe allegiance, and on whom ye pride yourselves, and whom ye mention by day and by night, and from whose traces ye seek guidance—had they lived in these days, they would have circled around Me, and would not have separated themselves from Me, whether at eventide or at morn. Ye, however, did not turn your faces towards My face, for even less than a moment, and waxed proud, and were careless of this Wronged One, Who hath been so afflicted by men that they dealt with Him as they pleased. Ye failed to inquire about My condition, nor did ye inform yourselves of the things which befell Me. Thereby have ye withheld from yourselves the winds of holiness, and the breezes of bounty, that blow from this luminous and perspicuous Spot. Methinks ye have clung to outward things, and forgotten the inner things, and say that which ye do not. Ye are lovers of names, and appear to have given yourselves up to them. For this reason make ye mention of the names of your leaders. And should any one like them, or superior unto them, come unto you, ye would flee him. Through their names ye have exalted yourselves, and have secured your positions, and live and prosper. And were your leaders to reappear, ye would not renounce your leadership, nor would ye turn in their direction, nor set your faces towards them. We found you, as We found most men, worshipping names which they mention during the days of their life, and with which they occupy themselves. No sooner do the Bearers of these names appear, however, than they repudiate them, and turn upon their heels. . . . Know ye that God will not, in this day, accept your thoughts, nor your remembrance of Him, nor your turning towards Him, nor your devotions, nor your vigilance, unless ye be made new in the estimation of this Servant, could ye but perceive it.

Because of you the Apostle (Muḥammad) lamented, and the Chaste One (Fáṭimih) cried out, and the countries were laid waste, and darkness fell upon all regions. O concourse of divines! Because of you the people were abased, and the banner of Islám was hauled down, and its mighty throne subverted. Every time a man of discernment hath sought to hold fast unto that which would exalt Islám, you raised a clamour, and thereby was He deterred from achieving His purpose, while the land remained fallen in clear ruin.

Of all the peoples of the world, they that have suffered the greatest loss have been, and are still, the people of Persia. I swear by the Day Star of Utterance which shineth upon the world in its meridian glory! The lamentations of the pulpits, in that country, are being raised continually. In the early days such lamentations were heard in the Land of Tá (Ṭihrán), for pulpits, erected for the purpose of remembering the True One—exalted be His glory—have now, in Persia, become places wherefrom blasphemies are uttered against Him Who is the Desire of the worlds.

In this day the world is redolent with the fragrances of the robe of the Revelation of the Ancient King . . . and yet, they (divines) have gathered together, and established themselves upon their seats, and have spoken that which would put an animal to shame, how much more man himself! Were they to become aware of one of their acts, and perceive the mischief it hath wrought, they would, with their own hands, dispatch themselves to their final abode.

O CONCOURSE of divines! . . . Lay aside that which ye possess, and hold your peace, and give ear, then, unto that which the Tongue of Grandeur and Majesty speaketh. How many the veiled handmaidens who turned unto Me, and believed, and how numerous the wearers of the turban who were debarred from Me, and followed in the footsteps of bygone generations!

O HIGH priests! Ears have been given you that they may hearken unto the mystery of Him Who is the Self-Dependent, and eyes that they may behold Him. Wherefore flee ye? The Incomparable Friend is manifest. He speaketh that wherein lieth salvation. Were ye, O high priests, to discover the perfume of the rose-garden of understanding, ye would seek none other but Him, and would recognize, in His new vesture, the All-Wise and Peerless One, and would turn your eyes from the world and all who seek it, and would arise to help Him.

Whatsoever hath been announced in the Books hath been revealed and made clear. From every direction the signs have been manifested. The Omnipotent One is calling, in this Day, and announcing the appearance of the Supreme Heaven.

This is not the day whereon the high priests can command and exercise their authority. In your Book it is stated that the high priests will, on that Day, lead men far astray, and will prevent them from drawing nigh unto Him. He indeed is a high priest who hath seen the light and hastened unto the way leading to the Beloved.

O high priests! The Hand of Omnipotence is stretched forth from behind the clouds; behold ye it with new eyes. The tokens of His majesty and greatness are unveiled; gaze ye on them with pure eyes.... Say, O high priests! Ye are held in reverence because of My Name, and yet ye flee Me! Ye are the high priests of the Temple. Had ye been the high priests of the Omnipotent One, ye would have been united with Him, and would have recognized Him. . . . Say, O high priests! No man's acts shall be acceptable, in this Day, unless he forsaketh mankind and all that men possess, and setteth his face towards the Omnipotent One.

THE GREAT ANNOUNCEMENT TO MANKIND

The time fore-ordained unto the peoples and kindreds of the earth is now come. The promises of God, as recorded in the holy Scriptures, have all been fulfilled. Out of Zion hath gone forth the Law of God, and Jerusalem, and the hills and land thereof, are filled with the glory of His Revelation. Happy is the man that pondereth in his heart that which hath been revealed in the Books of God, the Help in Peril, the Self-Subsisting. Meditate upon this, O ye beloved of God, and let your ears be attentive unto His Word, so that ye may, by His grace and mercy, drink your fill from the crystal waters of constancy, and become as steadfast and immovable as the mountain in His Cause.

Verily I say, this is the Day in which mankind can behold the Face, and hear the Voice, of the Promised One. The Call of God hath been raised, and the light of His countenance hath been lifted up upon men. It behoveth every man to blot out the trace of every idle word from the tablet of his heart, and to gaze, with an open and unbiased mind, on the signs of His Revelation, the proofs of His Mission, and the tokens of His glory.

Great indeed is this Day! The allusions made to it in all

the sacred Scriptures as the Day of God attest its greatness. The soul of every Prophet of God, of every Divine Messenger, hath thirsted for this wondrous Day. All the divers kindreds of the earth have, likewise, yearned to attain it. No sooner, however, had the Day Star of His Revelation manifested itself in the heaven of God's Will, than all, except those whom the Almighty was pleased to guide, were found dumbfounded and heedless.

O thou that hast remembered Me! The most grievous veil hath shut out the peoples of the earth from His glory, and hindered them from hearkening to His call. God grant that the light of unity may envelop the whole earth, and that the seal, 'the Kingdom is God's', may be stamped upon the brow of all its peoples.

O YE children of men! The fundamental purpose animating the Faith of God and His Religion is to safeguard the interests and promote the unity of the human race, and to foster the spirit of love and fellowship amongst men. Suffer it not to become a source of dissension and discord, of hate and enmity. This is the straight Path, the fixed and immovable foundation. Whatsoever is raised on this foundation, the changes and chances of the world can never impair its strength, nor will the revolution of countless centuries undermine its structure. Our hope is that the world's religious leaders and the rulers thereof will unitedly arise for the reformation of this age and the rehabilitation of its fortunes. Let them, after meditating on its needs, take counsel together and, through anxious and full deliberation, administer to a diseased and sorely-afflicted world the remedy it requires.... It is incumbent upon them who are in authority to exercise moderation in all things. Whatsoever passeth beyond the limits of moderation will cease to exert a beneficial influence. Consider for instance such things as liberty, civilization and the like. However much men of understanding may favourably regard them, they will, if carried to excess, exercise a pernicious influence upon men.... Please God, the peoples of the world may be led, as the result of the high endeavours exerted by their rulers and the wise and learned amongst men, to recognize their best interests. How long will humanity persist in its waywardness? How long will injustice continue? How long is chaos and confusion to reign amongst men? How long will discord agitate the face of society? The winds of despair are, alas, blowing from every direction, and the strife that divideth and afflicteth the human race is daily increasing. The signs of impending convulsions and chaos can now be discerned, inasmuch as the prevailing order appeareth to be lamentably defective. I beseech God, exalted be His glory, that He may graciously awaken the peoples of the earth, may grant that the end of their conduct may be profitable unto them, and aid them to accomplish that which beseemeth their station.

O CONTENDING peoples and kindreds of the earth! Set your faces towards unity, and let the radiance of its light shine upon you. Gather ye together, and for the sake of God resolve to root out whatever is the source of contention amongst you. Then will the effulgence of the world's great Luminary envelop the whole earth, and its inhabitants become the citizens of one city, and the occupants of one and the same throne. This wronged One hath, ever since the early days of His life, cherished none other desire but this, and will continue to entertain no wish except this wish. There can be no doubt whatever that the peoples of the world, of whatever race or religion, derive their inspiration from one heavenly Source, and are the subjects of one God. The difference between the ordinances under which they abide should be attributed to the varying requirements and exigencies of the age in which they were revealed. All of them, except a few which are the outcome of human perversity, were ordained of God, and are a reflection of His Will and Purpose. Arise and, armed with the power of faith, shatter to pieces the gods of your vain imaginings, the sowers of dissension amongst you. Cleave unto that which draweth you together and uniteth you. This, verily, is the most exalted Word which the Mother Book hath sent down and revealed unto you. To this beareth witness the Tongue of Grandeur from His habitation of glory.

THE GREAT ANNOUNCEMENT TO MANKIND

The Great Being, wishing to reveal the prerequisites of the peace and tranquillity of the world and the advancement of its peoples, hath written: The time must come when the imperative necessity for the holding of a vast, an all-embracing assemblage of men will be universally realized. The rulers and kings of the earth must needs attend it, and, participating in its deliberations, must consider such ways and means as will lay the foundations of the world's Great Peace amongst men. Such a peace demandeth that the Great Powers should resolve, for the sake of the tranquillity of the peoples of the earth, to be fully reconciled among themselves. Should any king take up arms against another, all should unitedly arise and prevent him. If this be done, the nations of the world will no longer require any armaments, except for the purpose of preserving the security of their realms and of maintaining internal order within their territories. This will ensure the peace and composure of every people, government and nation. We fain would hope that the kings and rulers of the earth, the mirrors of the gracious and almighty name of God, may attain unto this station, and shield mankind from the onslaught of tyranny.... The day is approaching when all the peoples of the world will have adopted one universal language and one common script. When this is achieved, to whatsoever city a man may journey, it shall be as if he were entering his own home. These things are obligatory and absolutely essential. It is incumbent upon every man of insight and understanding to strive to translate that which hath been written into reality and action.... That one indeed is a man who, today, dedicateth himself to the service of the entire human race. The Great Being saith: Blessed and happy is he that ariseth to promote the best interests of the peoples and kindreds of the earth. In another passage He hath proclaimed: It is not for him to pride himself who loveth his own country, but rather for him who loveth the whole world. The earth is but one country, and mankind its citizens.

The All-Knowing Physician hath His finger on the pulse of mankind. He perceiveth the disease, and prescribeth, in His unerring wisdom, the remedy. Every age hath its own problem, and every soul its particular aspiration. The remedy the world needeth in its present-day afflictions can never be the same as that which a subsequent age may require. Be anxiously concerned with the needs of the age ye live in, and centre your deliberations on its exigencies and requirements.

We can well perceive how the whole human race is encompassed with great, with incalculable afflictions. We see it languishing on its bed of sickness, sore-tried and disillusioned. They that are intoxicated by self-conceit have interposed themselves between it and the Divine and infallible Physician. Witness how they have entangled all men, themselves included, in the mesh of their devices. They can neither discover the cause of the disease, nor have they any knowledge of the remedy. They have conceived the straight to be crooked, and have imagined their friend an enemy.

Incline your ears to the sweet melody of this Prisoner. Arise, and lift up your voices, that haply they that are fast asleep may be awakened. Say: O ye who are as dead! The Hand of Divine bounty proffereth unto you the Water of Life. Hasten and drink your fill. Whoso hath been re-born in this Day, shall never die; whoso remaineth dead, shall never live.

O PEOPLES of the earth! God, the Eternal Truth, is My witness that streams of fresh and soft-flowing waters have gushed from the rocks, through the sweetness of the words uttered by your Lord, the Unconstrained; and still ye slumber. Cast away that which ye possess, and, on the wings of detachment, soar beyond all created things. Thus biddeth you the Lord of creation, the movement of Whose Pen hath revolutionized the soul of mankind.

Know ye from what heights your Lord, the All-Glorious is calling? Think ye that ye have recognized the Pen wherewith your Lord, the Lord of all names, commandeth you?

Nay, by My life! Did ye but know it, ye would renounce the world, and would hasten with your whole hearts to the presence of the Well-Beloved. Your spirits would be so transported by His Word as to throw into commotion the Greater World—how much more this small and petty one! Thus have the showers of My bounty been poured down from the heaven of My loving-kindness, as a token of My grace; that ye may be of the thankful. . . .

Beware lest the desires of the flesh and of a corrupt inclination provoke divisions among you. Be ye as the fingers of one hand, the members of one body. Thus counselleth you the Pen of Revelation, if ye be of them that believe.

Consider the mercy of God and His gifts. He enjoineth upon you that which shall profit you, though He Himself can well dispense with all creatures. Your evil doings can never harm Us, neither can your good works profit Us. We summon you wholly for the sake of God. To this every man of understanding and insight will testify.

THE world's equilibrium hath been upset through the vibrating influence of this most great, this new World Order. Mankind's ordered life hath been revolutionized through the agency of this unique, this wondrous System—the like of which mortal eyes have never witnessed.

Immerse yourselves in the ocean of My words, that ye

may unravel its secrets, and discover all the pearls of wisdom that lie hid in its depths. Take heed that ye do not vacillate in your determination to embrace the truth of this Cause—a Cause through which the potentialities of the might of God have been revealed, and His sovereignty established. With faces beaming with joy, hasten ye unto Him. This is the changeless Faith of God, eternal in the past, eternal in the future. Let him that seeketh, attain it; and as to him that hath refused to seek it—verily, God is Self-Sufficient, above any need of His creatures.

Say: This is the infallible Balance which the Hand of God is holding, in which all who are in the heavens and all who are on the earth are weighed, and their fate determined, if ye be of them that believe and recognize this truth. Say: Through it the poor have been enriched, the learned enlightened, and the seekers enabled to ascend unto the presence of God. Beware, lest ye make it a cause of dissension amongst you. Be ye as firmly settled as the immovable mountain in the Cause of your Lord, the Mighty, the Loving.

O YE peoples of the world! Know assuredly that My commandments are the lamps of My loving providence among My servants, and the keys of My mercy for My creatures. Thus hath it been sent down from the heaven of the Will of your Lord, the Lord of Revelation. Were any man to taste the sweetness of the words which the lips of the All-Merciful have willed to utter, he would, though the treasures of the earth be in his possession, renounce them one and all, that he might vindicate the truth of even one of His commandments, shining above the Dayspring of His bountiful care and loving-kindness.

From My laws the sweet smelling savour of My garment can be smelled, and by their aid the standards of victory will be planted upon the highest peaks. The Tongue of My power hath, from the heaven of My omnipotent glory, addressed to My creation these words: 'Observe My commandments, for the love of My beauty.' Happy is the lover that hath inhaled the divine fragrance of his Best-Beloved from these words, laden with the perfume of a grace which no tongue can describe. By My life! He who hath drunk the choice wine of fairness from the hands of My bountiful favour, will circle around My commandments that shine above the Dayspring of My creation.

Think not that We have revealed unto you a mere code of laws. Nay, rather, We have unsealed the choice Wine with the fingers of might and power. To this beareth witness that which the Pen of Revelation hath revealed. Meditate upon this, O men of insight! . . .

Whenever My laws appear like the sun in the heaven of Mine utterance, they must be faithfully obeyed by all, though My decree be such as to cause the heaven of every religion to be cleft asunder. He doth what He pleaseth. He chooseth; and none may question His choice. Whatsoever He, the Well-Beloved, ordaineth, the same is, verily, beloved. To this He Who is the Lord of all creation beareth Me witness. Whoso hath inhaled the sweet fragrance of the All-Merciful, and recognized the Source of this utterance, will welcome with his own eyes the shafts of the enemy, that he may establish the truth of the laws of God amongst men. Well is it with him that hath turned thereunto, and apprehended the meaning of His decisive decree.

This is the Day in which God's most excellent favours have been poured out upon men, the Day in which His most mighty grace hath been infused into all created things. It is incumbent upon all the peoples of the world to reconcile their differences, and, with perfect unity and peace, abide beneath the shadow of the Tree of His care and loving-kindness. It behoveth them to cleave to whatsoever will, in this Day, be conducive to the exaltation of their stations, and to the promotion of their best interests. Happy are those whom the all-glorious Pen was moved to remember, and blessed are those men whose names, by virtue of Our inscrutable decree, We have preferred to conceal.

Beseech ye the one true God to grant that all men may be graciously assisted to fulfil that which is acceptable in

Our sight. Soon will the present-day order be rolled up, and a new one spread out in its stead. Verily, thy Lord speaketh the truth, and is the Knower of things unseen.

REFERENCES

References

Abbreviations

Aq. Kitáb-i-Aqdas, the Most Holy Book.

ESW. Epistle to the Son of the Wolf (Bahá'í Publishing Trust, Wilmette; 1949).

Gl. Gleanings from the Writings of Bahá'u'lláh (Bahá'í Publishing Trust, Wilmette; 1963).

PDC. The Promised Day Is Come, Shoghi Effendi (Bahá'í Publishing Trust, Wilmette; 1941).

SM. Súriy-i-Mulúk (Tablet to the Kings, quoted in various works).

QV. Tablet to Queen Victoria.

Page

v Part of the record by E. G. Browne, the orientalist, of the words addressed to him by Bahá'u'lláh on the occasion of Browne's visit to Him in Bahjí in 1890. (See Browne, *A Traveller's Narrative*, Introduction, p. xl, Cambridge University Press, 1891).

5 Aq. cited Gl. cv; the last paragraph of this passage beginning 'We have asked nothing from you. . .' is taken from the Kitáb-i-Aqdas and is cited in PDC. page 26.

7 The whole of this passage beginning 'O Kings of the earth. . .' is taken from the Súriy-i-Mulúk, the first paragraph being cited in PDC. 20/21, the next four paragraphs in Gl. cxviii and the last three paragraphs in Gl. cxvi. ('Thy' in the last para. refers to Bahá'u'lláh).

12 QV. cited Gl. cxix.

13 Cited Gl. cii.

17 Tablet to Napoleon III cited ESW. 46 et seq.

27 Tablet to Czar Alexander II cited PDC. 32.

33 Tablet to Queen Victoria cited PDC. 34. cf. pp. 12, 67.

39 To Kaiser Wilhelm I; Aq. cited PDC. 36.
43 To Emperor Francis Joseph; Aq. cited PDC. 37.
47 Tablet to Sulṭán 'Abdu'l-'Azíz; SM. cited Gl. cxiv.
57 Tablet to Náṣiri'd-Dín Sháh cited PDC. 40.
63 To the Rulers of America; Aq. cited Citadel of Faith 18.
67 QV. cited Gl. cxx.
73 Aq. cited Gl. xcviii.
74 Passage beginning 'O concourse of divines. . .' and the following four passages cited PDC. 84, 85, 86.
79 The four passages beginning 'Those divines . . . who are truly . . .' cited PDC. 115.
80 Passage beginning 'O concourse of divines! Ye shall not. . .' cited PDC. 84.
83 Tablet to Pope Pius IX cited PDC. 30.
87 Cited PDC. 78.
89 'Call out to Zion, O Carmel, . . .' Tablet of Carmel cited Gl. xi.
89 'The Most Great Law is come. . .' cited PDC. 78.
90 'The Breath hath been wafted. . .' cited PDC. 79.
90 'Lend an ear unto. . .' cited ESW. 144.
91 'O concourse of Christians! We have. . .' cited PDC. 109/110.
92 'We, verily, have come. . .' cited PDC. 110.
92 Four passages addressed to patriarchs, archbishops and bishops (two) cited PDC. 104, 105.
94 Two passages addressed 'O concourse of priests. . .' cited PDC. 105.
95 'O concourse of monks. . .'; Tablet to Napoleon III, repeated in ESW. 49, cited PDC. 106.
96 'O concourse of monks. . .' cited PDC. 106.
97 'Consider, likewise, how numerous. . .' cited PDC. 107.
97 'Read ye the Evangel. . .' cited PDC. 107.
98 Cited Gl. xviii, 4th para.

REFERENCES

99   Cited Gl. xvii.
101 'O concourse of Persian divines...' cited PDC. 92.
102 'O ye divines of the City...'; SM. cited PDC. 92.
103 'Because of you the Apostle...' cited PDC. 91.
104 'Of all the peoples of the world...' cited PDC. 90.
104 'In this day the world is redolent...' PDC. 91.
105 'O concourse of divines...' cited PDC. 91.
105 'O high priests...' cited PDC. 79.
106 'Whatsoever hath been announced...' PDC. 79.
106 'This is not the day...' cited PDC. 80.
106 'O high priests...' cited PDC. 80.
111 'The time fore-ordained...' cited Gl. x.
111 'Verily I say, this is the Day...' cited Gl. vii.
112 'O ye children of men...' cited Gl. cx.
114 'O contending peoples...' cited Gl. cxi.
115 'The Great Being...' cited Gl. cxvii.
116 'The All-Knowing Physician...' cited Gl. cvi.
117 'O peoples of the earth...'; Aq. cited Gl. lxxii.
118 'The world's equilibrium...'; Aq. cited Gl. lxx.
119 'O ye peoples of the world...'; Aq. cited Gl. clv.
121 'This is the day...' cited Gl. iv.